University College Worcester
Library
Henwick Grove, WORC
D1461042

GCSE Citizenship Studies *for* AQA

The Peirson Library
UNIVERSITY COLLEGE WORCESTER
Henwick Grove, Worcester, WR2 6AJ
Telephone: 01905 855341

Return on or before the last date stamped below.

RESOURCE AREA

05 DEC 2004
CANCELLED

19 MAY 2005

Joan Campbell • Sue Patrick

Heinemann

Heinemann Educational Publishers
Halley Court, Jordan Hill, Oxford, OX2 8EJ
Part of Harcourt Education
Heinemann is the registered trademark of Harcourt Education Limited

© 2002 Joan Campbell, Sue Patrick

Copyright notice
All rights reserved. No part of this publication may be reproduced in any material form (including photocopying or storing it in any medium by electronic means and whether or not transiently or incidentally to some other use of this publication) without the prior written permission of the copyright owner, except in accordance with the provisions of the Copyright, Designs and Patents Act 1988 or under the terms of a licence issued by the Copyright Licensing Agency Ltd, 90 Tottenham Court Road, London W1P 0LP. Applications for the copyright owner's written permission to reproduce any part of this publication should be addressed to the publisher.

First published 2002

ISBN 0 435 80810 9

06 05 04
10 9 8 7 6 5 4 3 2

UNIVERSITY COLLEGE WORCESTER LIBRARY
NO9092
School Resource Area
323.
6
CAM

Edited by Phebe Kynaston

Designed by Hicksdesign

Typeset and illustrated by Gecko Limited

Original illustrations © Harcourt Education Limited, 2002

Printed and bound in Spain by Edelvives

Acknowledgements
The publishers would like to thank the following for permission to reproduce copyright material.

Maps and extracts
p. 11 @*The Guardian*, Clare Dyer, 20 March 2002; **p. 26** 1.5, 1.6 *Kick it Out*, October 2001; **p. 40** Nissan Motor Manufacturing (UK) Ltd; p. @*The Observer*, Neasa MacErlean, 24 February 2002; **p. 102** @Daily Mirror, 11 March 2002; **p. 102** @*Daily Mirror*, 'Voice of the Mirror' 13 March 2002; **p. 104** @*Daily Mirror*, James Hardy 16 March 2002; **p. 105** @*The Guardian*, Ian Black, 16 March 2002; **p. 109** Christian Aid; **p. 109** @*The Guardian*, John Pilger, 4 March 2002; **p. 133** Greenpeace; **p. 133** @*The Times*, Robert Whymant, 23 March 2002.

Photographs
p. 7, 8 John Walmsley **p. 7, 8** Ace Photoagency **p. 7** Sally & Richard Greenhill/Sally Greenhill **p. 10** Popperfoto **p. 11** Sipa Press/Rex Features **p. 12** Sally & Richard Greenhill **p. 13** John Walmsley **p. 15** Rex Features **p. 15** Popperfoto/Paul Bates/Reuters **p. 15, 8** Sipa Press/Rex Features **p. 15** Popperfoto/Reuters **p. 15** Rex Features/ Michael Powell **p. 18** Ace Photoagency **p. 19** Rex Features/Tim Rooke **p. 22** John Walmsley **pp. 26, 150** Empics/Matthew Ashton **p. 26** Empics/Neal Simpson **p. 29** Rex Features **p. 30** Rex Features **p. 31** Impact/Tony Page **p. 34, 150** Popperfoto **p. 35** Alamy/Peter Bowater **p. 39** Nissan Motor Manufacturing (UK) Ltd **p. 41** Popperfoto **p. 45** Impact/Robin Lawrence **p. 45** Rex Features **p. 45** Impact/Alain Evrard **p. 46** Impact/Martin Black **p. 46** Impact/Simon Shepheard **p. 52, 4** Rex Features **p. 53** Rex Features **p. 56** Popperfoto **p. 132** Greenpeace **p. 54** Choose: John Searle **p. 55** Popperfoto **p. 56, 4** Network/Justin Leighton **p. 61** Popperfoto **p. 48** Sally & Richard Greenhill **p. 62, 60** Impact/Petteri Kokkonen **p. 66** Choose: Adam Woolfit **p. 68** Rex Features **p. 69, 60** Rex Features **p. 65, 150** Popperfoto **p. 49** Choose: Sally Greenhill **p. 72** Impact/Piers Cavendish **p. 74** Popperfoto **p. 77** Ace Photoagency/ Roger Howard **p. 77** Popperfoto **p. 80** Impact/Bruce Stephens **p. 80** Sally & Richard Greenhill **p. 81** Popperfoto **p. 82** Network/Jonathan Olley **p. 83** Sally & Richard Greenhill **p. 84, 150** Sally & Richard Greenhill **p. 85, 150** Network/Barry Lewis **p. 86** Network/Christopher Pillitz **p. 88** Impact/Peter Arkell **p. 14** Sally Greenhill **p. 90** Sally & Richard Greenhill **p. 91** Rex Features **p. 98** Sally & Richard Greenhill **p. 100, 60** Popperfoto **p. 101, 60** Still Pictures **p. 126** Rex Features/Brian Rasic **p. 109** Still Pictures **p. 110** Popperfoto **p. 111** Network/Gideon Mendel **p. 127** Rex Features **p. 139** Still Pictures **p. 141** Impact/Mark Henley **p. 112** Rex Features **p. 129** Impact/Mike McQueen **p. 135** Sally & Richard Greenhill **p. 137** Rex Features **p. p. p. 142** Impact/ Rupert Eames **p. 143** Impact/Simon Shepheard **p. 145** Rex Features **p. 37** Rex Features **p. 38** Acestock/Chris Middlebrook **p. 97** Corbis/Ric Ergenbright **p. 102** Impact/Brian Harris **p. 116, 108** Network/Anthony Suau **p. 117** Popperfoto **p. 117, 108** Impact/Alan Kedhane **p. 124** Rex Features **p. 124** Popperfoto **p. 125** Impact Photos **p. 131** Rex Features **p. 63** Popperfoto/Reuters **p. 71** Hulton Archive **p. 93** Popperfoto/Reuters **p. 129** Popperfoto **p. 138** Network/Gideon Mendel **p. 140** Popperfoto **p. 25** Commission for Racial Equality **p. 53** Network/Mike Goldwater **p. 114** Roger Scruton **p. 59** Impact/Piers Cavendish **p. 60** Choose: Reuters/Paul Hackett **p. 60** AP Photo/Jeff Widener **p. 107** Popperfoto **p. 108** Still Pictures **p. 108** SPL **p. 149** Network/Martin Mayer **p. 56** Ace Photoagency/ Michael Melia **p. 99, 4** Network/Chris Davies **p. 24** Popperfoto/Reuters **p. 27** John Walmsley **p. 44** Impact Photos /Peter Arkell **p. 42** Still Pictures/ Klaus Andrews **p. 36** Harcourt Index **p. 47** Robert Harding/Adina Tovy **p. 73** Sally & Richard Greenhill **p. 76** Rex Features/Simon Walker **p. 104** Popperfoto/Reuters **p. 4** Sally & Richard Greenhill **p. 113, 4** Rex Features/SIPA **p. 119** Popperfoto/Reuters **p. 134** Still Pictures/Mark Edwards **p. 8** Sally & Richard Greenhill **p. 8** Sally & Richard Greenhill

The publishers have made every effort to trace the copyright holders, but if they have inadvertently overlooked any, they will be pleased to make the necessary arrangements at the first opportunity

Picture research by Thelma Gilbert

Websites
On pages where you are asked to go to www.heinemann.co.uk/hotlinks to complete a task or down load information, please insert the code **8109P** at the website.

Contents

HAVERING
GREEN
PARTY
POOL GREEN

Introduction

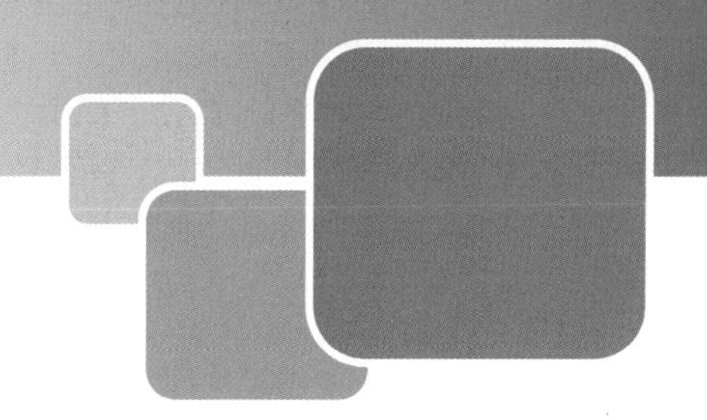

Studying to become a good citizen

This book aims to prepare you for the GCSE Short Course in Citizenship Studies. It encourages you to reflect on issues relating to your local community as well as national, European and global politics so you can formulate your own opinions after careful research and exploration of each issue. The course has three main topics:

- **Topic 1**: School, Work and the Local Community
- **Topic 2**: National and European Citizenship
- **Topic 3**: Global Citizenship.

In addition, the course has three themes:

- **Theme 1**: Rights and Responsibilities
- **Theme 2**: Decision-making, Power and Authority
- **Theme 3**: Participation in Citizenship Activities.

To do well with this course, you must:

- be prepared to undertake research
- discuss and debate issues in pairs and in groups
- take part in role-play activities to help you understand roles and the contribution of others
- undertake research using a variety of media, including the Internet and CD ROMs
- participate in school and community activities.

What are the values you need?

For yourself, you need to have good self-esteem, take responsibility for your own life and find some purpose in life.

In your relationships with others, you need to value others for themselves, care and respect other people regardless of age, religion, sex or culture, be loyal and trustworthy, be able to work co-operatively with others and resolve conflicts without recourse to violence.

As a member of society, you need to value truth and justice, respect and uphold a person's human rights, act responsibly as citizens respecting the law and the democratic process, promote equal opportunity for all and help those who are unable to support themselves.

As a global citizen, you should support sustainable developments to maximize the resources of the planet for the future, understand your responsibilities to other nations and their peoples and promote activities to support the balance and diversity in the world.

Developing personal skills

Building confidence

If you are confident about yourself, you will perform to the best of your ability in most situations. You won't feel silly about saying that you can't do something, you will know when to apologize for a mistake and you will not allow inappropriate peer comments to put you down.

To raise your confidence you should be:

- positive – think about issues carefully and look at life in a positive rather than a negative way.
- true to yourself – think about an issue and make up your own mind about how you feel about it and what you believe in.
- realistic – set yourself reasonable targets that you can achieve with perseverance and hard work.
- accepting – accept the point of view of others even if this is voiced as criticism of you, your work or your beliefs. If you are wrong, learn to apologize. This is not a sign of weakness.

- brave – have a go at new things. Even if they don't work, you'll know that you've tried. If they do work, it will give your confidence a boost!

Believing in yourself

Have a good opinion of yourself, know what your strengths are and use them. Good self-esteem will:

- make you feel confident in your thoughts and actions
- allow you to take risks and try new experiences
- help you believe in your own judgements
- help you in your relationships with other people
- help you to express your opinion openly and to accept that others may hold a different opinion to you.

Developing communication skills

Forming your own opinion

It is important when you enter into debates that you know the difference between an opinion and a fact. A fact is a true statement that has been experienced or observed. An opinion is a statement based on a particular point of view or on a feeling or belief. Before you take part in a discussion or debate:

- find out the facts – research your facts in books, articles and on the Internet
- note the arguments for and against the issue you are examining and identify the main points
- decide what your considered opinion is and make notes of the reasons why you hold that opinion.

Taking part in role-play situations

Role play and improvised drama allow you to explore someone else's reactions and views by standing in their shoes. When you are involved in role play you have to think very carefully about how the person you are representing would act, what they would say and how they would think in certain situations. You must become that person and act out your role in a way that is faithful to your new character.

Developing research and writing skills

Active research and case studies

Throughout this course you will need to spend time researching information to answer questions relating to your citizenship studies. You should keep a diary or notes of your research and its outcomes for future reference. Use the case studies to explore your feelings and attitudes to situations and issues which require you to think and act like a good citizen.

Developing your writing skills

Throughout your time at school you have been extending and developing your skill as a writer. In this course you should develop your style of writing because you will often be expressing your own views and feelings. To write an essay, article or report, you should:

- research your topic carefully
- make notes about the main facts and sources of your information
- make a plan by listing all the points you want to include
- state your viewpoint clearly in the opening paragraph, giving reasons for your opinions
- give evidence and examples from your own, and others' experiences, to support your statements
- end your writing with a statement which sums up your views and ideas, or resolves an argument if you are writing in a debating style.

When you have finished your piece of writing ask yourself the following questions:

- Does it have an effective opening?
- Are the main arguments supported by evidence?
- Does the writing keep the reader's interest?
- Does it have an appropriate ending?

If the answer to all of these questions is yes, then you have produced a good piece of writing.

School, work and the local community

Key ideas

Chapter 1 School

* Rights and responsibilities of parents, teachers and pupils
* Power and authority
* The school community
* The local community
* Equal opportunities

Chapter 2 Work

* Rights and responsibilities of employers and employees
* Health and safety
* The economy
* How do businesses use financial services
* Money matters – you and your money
* Types of business
* Industry sectors
* Work experience

Chapter 3 Local community

* Community life
* Local government
* Devolution – regional government in the UK
* Voting systems
* How individuals can bring about change

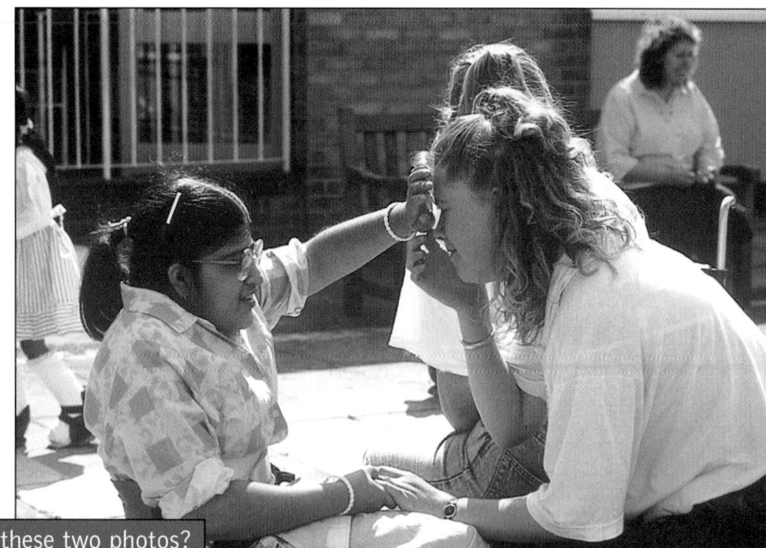

What rights and responsibilities, do you think, are being demonstrated in these two photos?

He fought peaceably to abolish apartheid for decades.
Sometimes fighting for your rights takes years of patient work.

What is work? Is it still work if you don't get paid for it? Do street corner musicians work

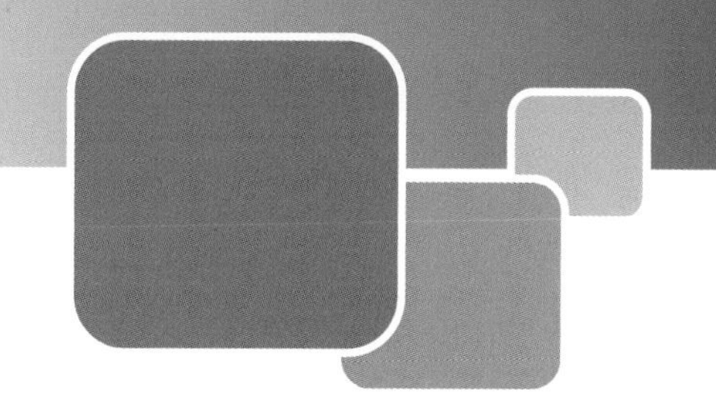

1 School

Rights and responsibilities

All rights bring some responsibility with them. The theme of rights and responsibilities runs throughout this course and you will read this phrase many times in this book. In the many roles we have in life, the term 'rights and responsibilities' will be used when referring to many people in a variety of situations. These people include children, parents, teachers, students, employers, employees, motorists, landlords and tenants.

Legal and moral rights

These rights and responsibilities may be legal or moral. **Legal** rights and responsibilities are what we can do and what we are responsible for according to the laws of the land. **Moral** rights and responsibilities are what we are expected to do according to the values of the society we live in. The **values** of a society are the things that are deemed to be worthwhile, are good and reflect society's expectations and conformity to a code of behaviour determined by the learned culture of that society.

Human rights

After World War II a group of nations formed the Council of Europe. This council formulated the European Convention for the Protection of Human Rights and Freedoms, now more usually referred to as the European Convention on Human Rights or the ECHR.

The Council of Europe consists of 39 states. It was established before the European Union and is completely separate from it. The purpose of the ECHR is to guarantee citizens of all the countries that have ratified (signed and agreed to) the convention sixteen basic definite human rights. These cover the right to

- liberty, including when liberty can be taken away
- justice
- privacy, family life and enjoyment of possessions
- education
- freedom of thought, expression, peaceful assembly and association
- freedom from slavery and forced labour.

These rights are safeguarded by the European Court of Human Rights in Strasbourg. Anyone who believes that their rights have been abused or violated by a government (not a company or an individual) and cannot gain justice in the courts of their home country can take their case to this court.

Usually the court sits with a Chamber (or panel) of nine judges, but sometimes a Grand Chamber of 21 judges can hear a complex case. The court decides if the convention has been broken or not, and has the power to make awards. The judgements (decisions) of the court are carried out by the Committee of Ministers of the Council of Europe. However, if the court decides that the convention has not been breached (broken), the case is closed and there is no appeal.

Activities

1. Make a list of the different groups that you belong to, for example family, youth club, etc.
2. What are your rights within each group you have identified?
3. What are your responsibilities within each group?
4. Do you think that any of these rights and responsibilities should be changed?

The UK was one of the original members of the Council of Europe and ratified the convention, but until 1998 there was no human rights legislation in the UK. The Human Rights Act 1998, which came into full force in October 2000, is 'an Act to give further effect to rights and freedoms guaranteed under the European Convention on Human Rights ...'

This means that claims can now be heard in British courts and do not have to go to Strasbourg. The Act sets out how the convention's rights are now applied to all British laws.

European judges in the Grand Chamber

Your rights under the Human Rights Act 1998 are taken from the following articles and protocols:

Article 2	Right to life
Article 3	Prohibition of torture
Article 4	Prohibition of slavery and forced labour
Article 5	Right to liberty and security
Article 6	Right to a fair trial
Article 7	Punishment must be lawful
Article 8	Right to respect for private and family life
Article 9	Freedom of thought, conscience and religion
Article 10	Freedom of expression
Article 11	Freedom of assembly and association
Article 12	Right to marry
Article 14	Prohibition of discrimination
Article 16	Restrictions on the political activity of aliens
Article 17	Prohibition of abuse of rights
Article 18	Limitation on use of restriction on rights
Article 1 of Protocol 1	Protection of property
Article 2 of Protocol 1	Right to education
Article 3 of Protocol 1	Right to free elections
Article 1 and 2 of Protocol 6	Abolition of the death penalty.

Case study

Diane Pretty makes final 'death with dignity' plea

Clare Dyer, legal correspondent, Guardian

WEDNESDAY 20 MARCH, 2002

Diane Pretty, the terminally ill woman who wants her husband to be allowed to help her commit suicide, made a final plea for the right to die with dignity at the European court of human rights yesterday.

The bench of seven judges in Strasbourg is Mrs Pretty's last hope after her plea was rejected by the high court, the court of appeal, and the House of Lords.

Paralysed from the neck down by motor neurone disease and with only months to live, she insisted on making the 12 hour journey from her home in Luton, Bedfordshire, through the Channel tunnel in a private ambulance with paramedics and an intensive care nurse in attendance ...

She listened intently as her QC, Philip Havers, argued that her 45-year-old husband should be allowed to help her take her life without fear of prosecution.

After the hearing Mrs Pretty, 43, who can speak only with the help of a voice synthesizer, said: 'I just want my rights.' ...

Jonathan Crow, representing the government, expressed sympathy for the 'tragic circumstances' of Mrs Pretty's case but said the law on assisted suicide was clear ...

The judges are expected to give their ruling within weeks.

Taken from the *Guardian*, 20 March 2002. Mrs Pretty died in a hospice on 11 May 2002.

Activities

Read the Case study and discuss the following:

1. Which human right formed the basis of Mrs Pretty's claim?
2. Why was she allowed to take her case to Strasbourg?
3. What is your opinion of all the judgements that have been made in this case?
4. Do you think there is ever a case for euthanasia?
5. In which European country is euthanasia legal?

Rights and responsibilities of children, parents, teachers and pupils

A right is something to which we are all entitled. Rights are sometimes called entitlements and sometimes freedoms under the ECHR. However, someone's right may be another person's responsibility, for example, a child has the right to love and care, which is usually the responsibility of the parents.

Children's rights

Children, especially young children, are some of the most vulnerable people in society and rely on their parents to protect and nurture them. In many parts of the world children's rights are being violated, for example some children work many hours a day in poor conditions for very low wages. In 1989 the United Nations drew up a Convention on the Rights of the Child, which became part of international law in 1992. For a convention to become part of international law it must be signed by at least 20 different countries. The main rights of the child that this tries to safeguard are for:

- food, health and a decent place to live
- free education and information
- freedom of thought, conscience and religion
- protection from slavery, exploitation and cruelty
- freedom to give their opinions on issues which affect them.

The rights of children in this country are now covered by the Children Act of 1989. This Act has the welfare of the child as its guiding principle, and the opinions of children are taken into account in a variety of situations by law.

Children's responsibilities

As children grow up these rights have responsibilities attached to them too, for example the right to education carries the responsibility of attending school regularly; freedom to express opinions carries the responsibility of allowing everyone to have their own opinions, even if they are not the same as yours. As children reach different ages they are allowed by law to become more responsible for their own actions.

Family time – eating a meal together

Parents' rights and responsibilities

Parents have the right to:

- choose the school they want their children to go to
- free education for their children between the ages of five and sixteen
- decide which religion their children are brought up in
- decide on discipline and punishments – this does not mean physical abuse
- choose medical treatment for their children.

Parents are responsible for the health and welfare and control of their children until they reach the age of eighteen. This means that parents make sure that their children:

- have a home to live in
- are fed, clothed and cared for
- receive proper medical treatment when they are ill
- attend school regularly.

They also control and exercise discipline and teach their children right from wrong.

If married parents separate or divorce and there is no agreement between them about the care of a child then a court will decide. The court has many powers and will consider all aspects of each case with the interests and welfare of the child uppermost, taking into account the age and opinions of the child.

Rights and responsibilities of pupils

Under the provisions of the Education Act 1997, parents are usually asked to sign a 'home–school' agreement when their children start attending a new school. This agreement sets out the main aims of the school and the shared responsibilities that home and school have for a pupil's education. A pupil is a person under the age of nineteen who is still attending school. A student is a person who is in full-time further or higher education.

Pupils have the right to:

- a safe working environment in which to learn
- good teaching
- be told of their progress and how they could improve where necessary.

Pupils helping each other to learn new skills

Pupils have the responsibility to:

- attend school regularly and on time
- behave reasonably and follow the school rules
- make sure they have all they need for lessons
- work hard and obey instructions
- respect other people, both pupils and teachers.

Rights and responsibilities of teachers

While pupils are in school teachers act 'in loco parentis' – which simply means in place of parents – to make sure that pupils are in a safe environment where they can learn.

The main responsibilities of teachers are:

- to keep up to date with their subject knowledge and the requirements of the National Curriculum
- to create a good learning environment in their classrooms and to teach effectively
- to create good relationships with pupils to encourage and support their learning
- to mark and assess pupils' work and highlight how improvements could be made
- to inform pupils and parents of progress or problems with learning
- to put into practice all the policies and procedures contained in the policy statements set out by the school. (These will differ from school to school, but all deal with how the school is organized and run and the procedures to be followed in a variety of different situations.)

Do teachers have any rights? Think about this for a while. It is probably something that has never occurred to you before.

Teachers have the right to:

- have a safe working environment
- expect pupils to behave reasonably and to work to the best of their ability
- have access to further training to be able to cater for the needs of pupils
- have access to new developments within their subject.

A Activities

1. Are the rights of pupils the same as the responsibilities of teachers?
2. Do all members of the school have a right to mutual trust and respect?
3. Are there any other rights or responsibilities you think should be included for children, parents, pupils or teachers?
4. Draw a chart to show the main rights and responsibilities of parents and children, and pupils and teachers.

Teacher and pupils working together

Power and authority

Defining power and authority

Power is the ability to influence or to rule. A group, such as a government, or an individual, such as a prime minister, can have the power to influence what happens and make changes.

Authority is a form of power which is accepted as a legal right to command or rule. Most people accept authority willingly. In a democracy people accept that Parliament makes laws which then have to be followed or obeyed.

Coercion is rule by force. Dictators rule by coercion – they do not offer people a choice.

Weber, an early sociologist, defined three types of authority which are still accepted today:

- **Legal (or legal–rational)** authority means people obey rules because they accept the law on which they are based. The laws are accepted because they achieve a common desired goal. People accept a person's authority because of their position in society, for example a policewoman.

Police officers

Nelson Mandela

- **Charismatic** authority is based upon the exceptional personal qualities of an individual. A charismatic leader is a person who has authority over others because of these special qualities, for example, Martin Luther King, a black civil rights leader in the USA in the 1960s. Such people can bring about change.
- **Traditional** authority is based on traditions that have been accepted for many, many years. In this case we accept the authority because it is the custom or because it was inherited, for example, the monarchy.

In practice power is most often exercised through the use of one or more forms of authority.

The Queen

Osama bin Laden

Tony Blair

Who has power and authority in schools?

Economic power

Who provides the money (funding) for schools? Economic power is a major influence in any organization. The government makes grants to local authorities, which also raise money from the council tax to pay for all local services. Education is one of the major costs to any council.

The Local Education Authority will allocate a budget (an amount of money) to each school. The school governors and head teacher are then responsible for managing the budget for their school and have the power to decide how to spend that money.

Activity

Look at the photographs on pages 15 and 16. Which type(s) of authority do these people have? Why?

Pupil power

Pupils may have some power too! Pupils of the same age will form friendship groups with others who have similar interests and who are in a similar situation. This is known as a peer group. Peer groups have a great influence on the individual; indeed some psychologists believe that it is the main influence on children and teenagers.

Think about the peer group that you belong to. Who are the other main members of that group? Are they about the same age? Do you have the same interests? What effect does your peer group have on you in terms of what you do, what clothes you choose, what music you like, how you spend your free time, your attitude to school? Does your peer group have a great effect on you?

There are other pupils in a school who exercise coercive power. They may be individuals or a small group – the bullies. They get what they want by threats or force of some kind. There are different forms of bullying and schools will try to prevent it.

Pupils may have another type of power if the school has year councils or a school council. Both would have elected representatives who would present the views and interests of their group. By discussion and negotiation some changes may be brought about.

Parent power

In choosing the most suitable school for their children, parents are fulfilling their responsibilities and exercising their power of choice. Schools which have a 'good reputation' will always be most popular and chosen more often. Parental choice is therefore very important to schools.

Parents have representatives on the governing body of the school. There may be a parent–teacher association with which parents can become involved to raise funds and also help the school in other ways.

School governors

The Education Reform Act 1988 set out the role of school governors. They have the power to establish the rules and regulations by which the school is governed in accordance with the Instruments of Government supplied by the local authority. School governors control the finances of the school including the money for buildings, salaries and equipment. They are responsible for order and discipline within the school.

Head teachers

The head teacher is the governors' agent within the school. The head teacher is responsible for managing every aspect of the school on a day-to-day basis in accordance with the governors' policies and practices.

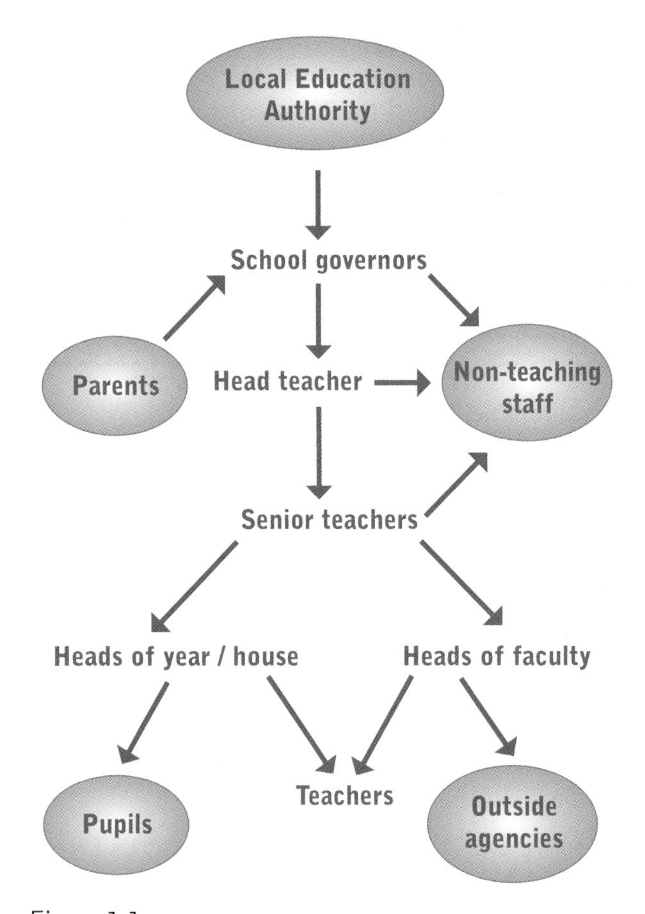

Figure 1.1

Activities

Figure 1.1 (page 17) shows how most schools are organized in terms of the main individuals and groups of people involved.

1 Using the flow chart discuss what type of power or authority each individual or group has.

2 Which people or groups may have more than one type of authority? Give reasons for your opinions.

The school community

Each school is a small community in which a number of people work together, share the same values and follow the same set of 'rules'. Each school has its own identity, although it will be similar to many other schools in a number of ways. For example, most schools have a uniform or a dress code (the similarity), but exactly what the uniform consists of or what colour it is will vary, giving a different identity.

As well as pupils and teachers, many other people make up the school community – secretaries, technicians, caretaking and cleaning staff, the school meals service, Education Welfare Officers, learning mentors, etc. Each person has a different, important role within the school community.

Within your school there will be many ways in which you learn about being a responsible adult. You may be given a specific task to be responsible for within your tutor group or form, such as collecting and returning the register for a week, month or term. A teacher may consider you to be reliable, responsible and trustworthy and ask you to collect homework from your group and take it to that teacher. You may have responsibilities within the year group, such as helping organize refreshments at a parents' evening. You may volunteer to be involved with a school play or concert, giving your time and effort to the school community.

Taking responsibility for doing even simple tasks and being reliable and completing the task is important and will be noticed and appreciated. As an adult in the wider community these characteristics are very important, especially in the world of work.

There will be many activities which pupils can participate in, which build up a sense of being a member of the school community. These activities could include:

- drama groups which produce school plays or Christmas pantomimes
- belonging to the school choir or orchestra
- representing the school in a sports team
- after-school clubs in computing or robotics.

A secondary school orchestra group, rehearsing

Many schools encourage their pupils to learn about the democratic process by the structured organization of the school. Your school may have a house system or year group system. Within both types of organization there would be a head of house or head of year, who is responsible for a number of pupils in a house or a year group. A year council may be set up with each tutor group electing one or two pupils to represent the group at year council meetings.

There may also be a school council with representatives elected from each year group. The elected members would hold meetings to discuss issues raised by pupils and teachers. By voting in such an election everyone is given the opportunity to participate in the democratic process in a small community.

Most schools will have just a few rules which are quite simple but make life much easier for the whole school community when they are followed (Figure 1.2).

Figure 1.2

Activities

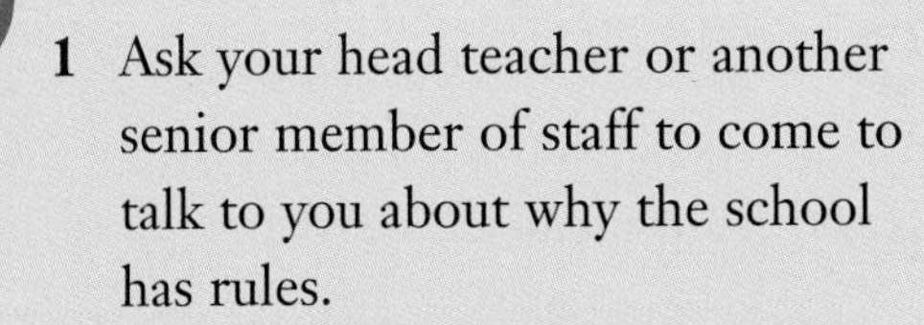

1 Ask your head teacher or another senior member of staff to come to talk to you about why the school has rules.
2 Who is responsible for making school rules and who is responsible for enforcing them?
3 Discuss your school rules and why they are important. What would happen if there were no school rules?

The school and the wider community

When a school invites local people outside the school community to take part in an event such as a summer fair or to watch a school play, a sense of belonging to a much wider community is developed.

A fund-raising or charity event can be an important way of building a sense of community spirit within both the school and the wider community. There is a great variety of activities you could organize to raise money for a local or national charity, for example Children in Need events take place all over the country each November. Those involved in such fund-raising usually enjoy it and a great number of children who are in need do benefit. Red Nose Day is another popular event. There may be a local charity which the school is involved with that would welcome extra funds.

Organizing a fund-raising event could also be your coursework project, but this would need a lot of discussion with your teacher and much planning before it could go ahead.

Organizing a fund-raising activity

For a successful fund-raising activity it is essential that you work with friends who you can trust and rely on to do their share of the work. It will involve a great deal of thinking, planning, organization, and co-operation within the group to make sure everything runs smoothly and within the timescale set.

- Begin by making a list of realistic activities that can be achieved within the time limits.
- Discuss your ideas and arrive at a decision.
- Talk to your teacher and gain approval for your chosen activity.
- In the group decide exactly what has to be done. (Remember that everyone must make a contribution, especially if this is for the assessed coursework. Each member of the group will probably have different skills to contribute.)
- Plan what has to be done and set dates by which the tasks have to be completed. This could be written up as a planning chart. Take into consideration what skills each person has to offer, for example using a computer to make good posters.

Children in Need's Pudsey Bear

- Discuss all your plans with your teacher and listen to any advice offered. Then having planned the event thoroughly, carry out all your plans.
- Write up your own account of the successful fund-raising activity. What to include:
  - Your plans showing the targets each person was set and when they had to be completed by. This could be a chart.
  - How successful was the event? Evaluate your contribution and that of the others in the group.
  - Who benefited from the activity?
  - How much did you raise? You could produce a balance sheet to show expenditure and income.
  - Did you enjoy the activity – why – why not?

Activities

1. Consider all the people who work in your school. Find out more about their responsibilities.
2. Make a list of all the different school clubs or groups which you could be involved with.
3. In small groups, make a list of fund-raising activities that you could organize. Discuss these with the rest of the class.
4. Discuss the following:
   - What makes your school a community?
   - Is your school democratic?
   - How does your school relate to the wider community?

The local community – where are U in your commUnity?

What is a community?

A community is made up of all the people who live in an area, as well as the facilities and services that exist in that location (see Figure 1.3). Some communities will have different buildings, houses, services and facilities from others, for example a rural area will be different from an urban area.

The council is responsible for providing services such as schools, libraries, parks and recreational services, police and fire services and council housing. Doctors and dentists are part of the health service and are known as primary care groups. Different faiths may have built their centres of worship such as churches, mosques and synagogues.

People may organize or join local groups that provide leisure, recreational or sporting and even educational activities, for example a youth club, five-a-side football teams, a luncheon club for elderly people or a playgroup. In this way a sense of community and belonging is developed.

Some community schools provide a range of activities for people in their community as well as offering educational courses and qualifications for adults. Sometimes adults join in the same lessons as pupils for some AS or GNVQ courses.

All of these types of activity develop a greater understanding between people of varying ages and encourage everyone to take more responsibility for their community, creating a sense of identity and belonging to that community.

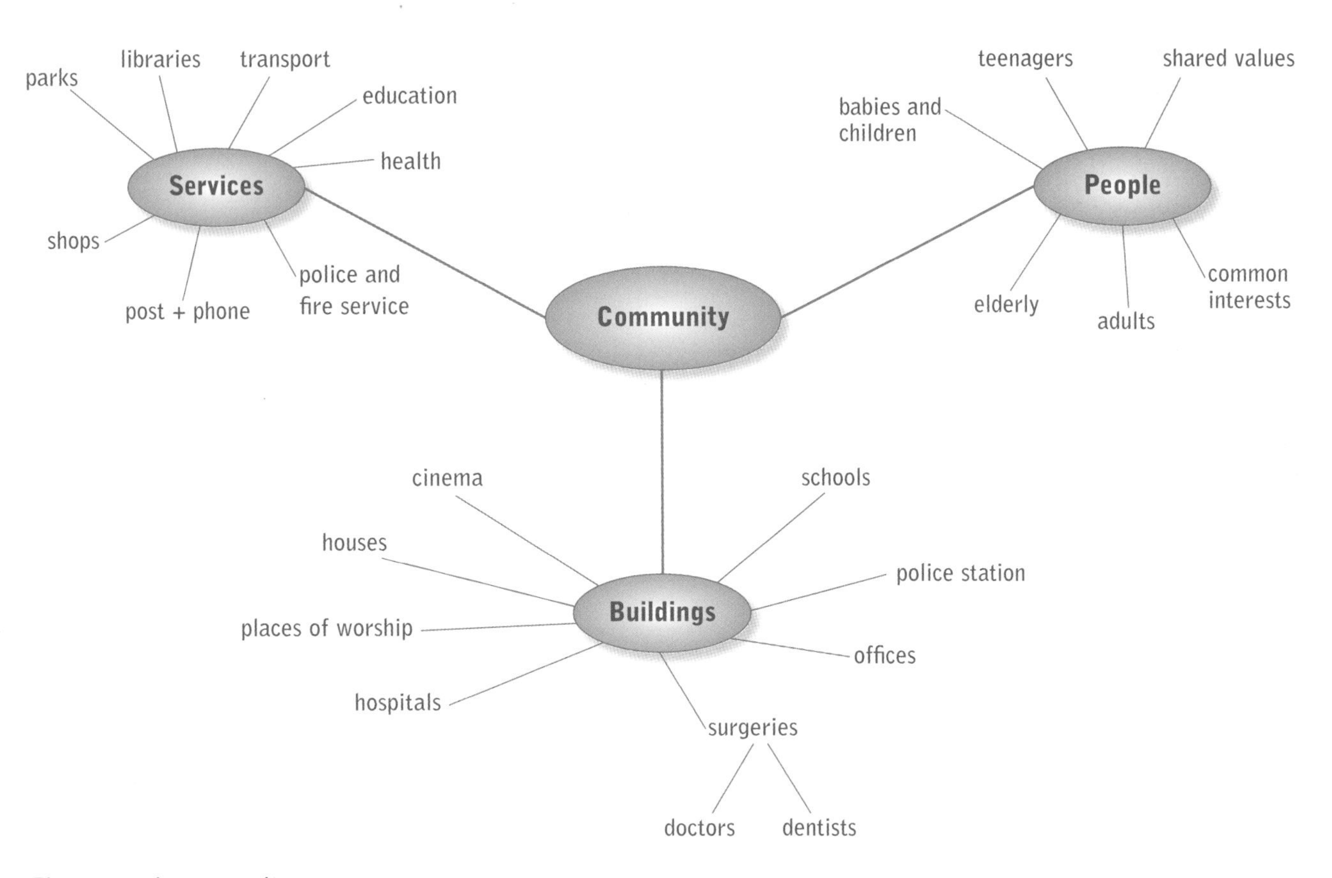

Figure 1.3 A community

Case study: The community and you

Activities

Read the case study and discuss the following questions:

1. Do the teenagers mean to disturb Mrs Smith?
2. Why does Mrs Smith feel intimidated?

Mrs Smith has moved into one of the bungalows surrounding the grassed play area. In the spring evenings a group of teenagers regularly gather outside and sit on her garden wall. Mrs Smith is intimidated by their behaviour because they play loud music and often shout and swear at each other. She is frightened to go out and speak to them.

In a community people care for and support others, such as very young children, the elderly and disabled people. We try to show understanding of people and realize that people of all races and religions have the same needs.

We try to think about how other people may feel and to understand other people's points of view. Do you think you are a responsible member of your community? Do you know people who are sometimes obstructive, dismissive, intolerant and selfish?

Have you ever been told that you have a 'bad attitude' or that you have 'an attitude problem'? Who told you this? Was it a parent, a teacher or a friend? What did that person actually mean? Did they mean that your behaviour was inappropriate at that time, or that it was completely unacceptable to others? Was that person right?

We have all heard comments like those in Figure 1.4. Sometimes people just don't stop to think about what they do or say, and the way this can affect others.

The way we behave really *does* affect other people. Being a good member of your community involves *you* taking responsibility for what *you* do.

Figure 1.4

Activities

1. List the different services and all the different types of buildings in your community.
2. On a map of the area around your school, highlight all the facilities available.
3. Name as many local groups or organizations as you can.
4. Which groups do you belong to?
5. What does your community do for you? What do you do for your community?

7. How is your school involved with the local community?
8. Look at Figure 1.4. In a small group, discuss the attitudes and the effect they might have on other people.

Equal opportunities

What do we mean by equal opportunities?

Most people would say that equal opportunities means there should be no discrimination on the grounds of gender, race, creed (religion), age or disability. In other words everyone should have an equal chance based on their ability and there should be fair treatment for all. No one should be discriminated against because they are different in some way.

There are many laws which try to enforce the principle of equal opportunity, and they have gone a long way towards creating more equal opportunities for many people. Unfortunately there are still many people who have stereotyped or what some call 'traditional' attitudes which need to be changed. This process of change will take time before there really is equality of opportunity for all.

One of the ways we can help to create more equality of opportunity is by starting in school, even nursery school (because children start learning from a very early age), and carrying on throughout education. In this way equality of opportunity will be expected at home and at work, and will eventually become an accepted part of our society. Equal opportunities can be promoted in many ways and we are going to examine some of these practices in schools.

During your education do you feel that you have had equal opportunities? Discuss this in a small group, then as a whole class. It may be useful to write down some of your thoughts and opinions as well as those of others in your group.

Equal opportunities at school

All areas of school should be equally welcoming to both boys and girls. Schools can promote equality of opportunity by ensuring that boys and girls are treated exactly the same. There should be no differences in the way good work and behaviour are rewarded. Members of staff should not accept bad behaviour from boys or girls, and no one should 'get away with' something because of their gender.

Displays around the school, teaching materials, visual aids, posters and books should show the diversity within our society and challenge stereotypes of any sort, thereby encouraging positive attitudes towards equality of opportunity regardless of gender, race, religion or disability.

Learning about equal opportunities often starts in school

Activities that can promote equal opportunities

Activities that could be organized for the whole school or just for a year group include:

- *a special equal opportunities day* – people from different trades and professions are invited into school to speak to groups of pupils to show how traditional roles are changing, for example women are becoming joiners and plumbers and men are becoming nurses and secretaries
- *a multicultural day/evening* – where different cultures are represented by people from those cultures in traditional dress who explain their customs and offer samples of foods
- *inviting speakers from different religions* – to talk to pupils
- *arranging visits* – to different places of worship.

A career fair at school – promoting opportunities at work

The school curriculum

In schools everyone must have equal access to all parts of the curriculum. When choices have to be made about which subjects to study for GCSE, teenagers should be encouraged to make decisions based on which subjects they have an aptitude for and an interest in. Career choices and advice should follow the same guidelines.

Activities

1. Obtain a copy of your school's Equal Opportunities Policy statement. Read it and discuss it in a small group.
2. Discuss how well you think this policy is carried out.
3. Find out more about the Equal Opportunities Commission (EOC) and the Sex Discrimination Act 1975; go to *www.heinemann.co.uk/hotlinks* and look at the EOC website.
4. Do you think that teenagers have 'traditional' stereotypical attitudes? Discuss in groups.
5. Explain what you understand by the following terms:

   a) equal opportunities

   b) gender bias

   c) stereotypes.
6. Write a short newspaper article on how equal opportunities may be encouraged at home and in school.

The Race Relations Act

The Race Relations Act 1976 established the Commission for Racial Equality (CRE). In 2000 the 1976 Act was amended by the Race Relations (Amendment) Act 2000.

The Commission for Racial Equality has three main functions:

- to try to eliminate racial discrimination and promote equality of opportunity
- to encourage good relations between peoples from different backgrounds
- to monitor the way the Act is working and make recommendations for improvements.

Your rights under the Race Relations Act

The Act makes it illegal for a person to be treated less favourably than others on the grounds of race, colour, nationality or ethnicity. The Race Relations (Amended) Act 2000 imposes duties on public authorities to promote racial equality in the areas of education, training, jobs, housing and services. It is a criminal offence to print and distribute material that is likely to incite racial hatred, which is dealt with by the police. Publishing racially offensive material in the media is not allowed. Complaints about material in newspapers are dealt with by the Press Complaints Commission, and complaints about adverts, by the Advertising Standards Authority.

A Commission for Racial Equality poster

THERE ARE LOTS OF PLACES IN BRITAIN WHERE RACISM DOESN'T EXIST.

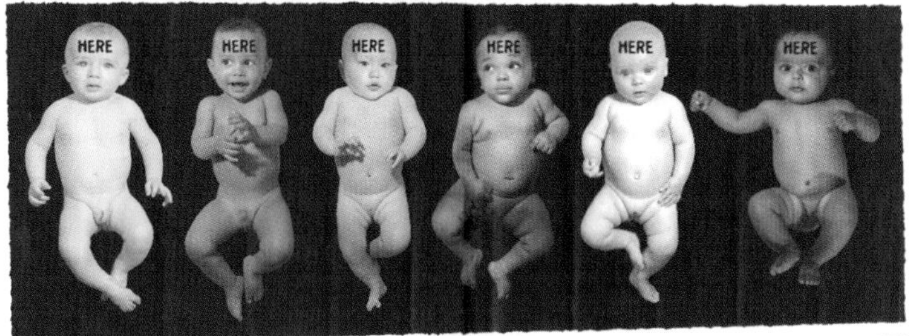

COMMISSION FOR RACIAL EQUALITY

What does all this mean?

1 Lisa is English. Her parents were born in England and her grandparents have taken English citizenship but came from Jamaica. Lisa and her parents want her to go to the local comprehensive school, but she has not been given a place there.

If this was because of her race what type of discrimination would this be? Would it be lawful? What should Lisa's parents do about it? Where could they get help?

2 Uptown School has different uniform rules for boys and girls. Girls are not allowed to wear trousers and boys are not allowed to wear any head covering.

Is this lawful? Do you think the school uniform policy is discrimination? Who might be affected and why? What can be done about it?

What is discrimination?

'Discrimination can be of two types (see also pages 78, 79):

i) **Direct racial discrimination** is when a person is treated less favourably on racial grounds than others in similar circumstances.

ii) **Indirect racial discrimination** is when people from a particular group are less likely to be able to comply with a requirement, and the requirement cannot be justified on non-racial grounds.' (From the Commission for Racial Equality)

What is racism?
Racism is a belief that people of a particular race or ethnic group are inferior or superior. This is most often due to prejudice.

What is racial prejudice?
Racial prejudice is the forming of a personal opinion or judgement about an ethnic group or race without real knowledge of that group or race. This is not the same as racial discrimination.

Equal opportunities in sport

Hope for England

Three years ago Hope Powell became the first black coach to take charge of England – the women's team, that is.

You are not only the first woman and the youngest person to manage an England side, but the first black person. How did it feel when you were told?

I think I experienced every emotion. I was overwhelmed at first. It was very exciting but a bit scary too. Then I thought 'This is a once in a lifetime opportunity, I've got to do it.'

Being young, female and black I knew I could be a positive role model for young people. I hope I can help some young black people in particular to believe in themselves and strive to be the best. I want to succeed for myself and, as the first black player in such a senior position, I want to do it for everyone else as well.

Did your family support you in your career?

My mother is West Indian and there's a very different culture there so it was a bit difficult for her to understand why a girl would want to play football. It doesn't happen in Jamaica. Now my Mum is quite proud, especially after I got this job and there was so much media coverage.

Did you experience racism in women's football when you were playing?

I remember one game when I was quite young and someone referred to me as a 'black bastard' or something. Luckily my teammate heard and she went absolutely berserk – she was five years older than me. Later when I was playing for England in Croatia this boy, he was only 12, made a Nazi salute at me. I couldn't believe it but I didn't react.

Figure 1.5 Hope Powell became manager of the England women's team in 1998, from *Kick It Out* magazine, October 2001

Education is the answer *says* Manchester United *boss Sir Alex Ferguson*

You're known as a great motivator. How do you motivate young black players to overcome racism?

All people will come up against barriers in life. The first thing you think is 'I don't deserve this.' But you have to be determined to overcome it. You've got to have a sort of blinkered approach to it, and think, 'This is not going to stop me.'

The situation today is better than it was 20 years ago, and 20 years ago it was better than 30 years ago. So progress eventually eliminates a lot of what is going on. But when the prejudice stops people getting a job, puts them out of a job, or stops them getting a place on the team because of their colour, that is real racism to me.

If you had the power to change things what would you want to change?

I think it's all down to education and how people are brought up. I was brought up in a family where there was never any prejudice. I think education from the family and school are the most important things. If parents are saying to their kids 'Don't play with that Charlie down the road because he is black,' what message does that give? I think education is the secret.

Figure 1.6 From *Kick It Out* magazine, October 2001

Children, developing their skills in athletics

Activities

1 'The Equal Opportunities Commission believes it is wrong that girls who are fit and able to participate in a sport, and capable on their own merits to play in teams, should be banned from taking part in activities they choose. Girls should have the same rights as boys to develop their skills.' (From the Equal Opportunities Commission website.)

The instructions to schools from the Football Association prohibit girls and boys over eleven years of age from playing in the same team because football is a contact sport.

Discuss these two points of view.

2 Using a word processor, write an article for a sports page of your school magazine about racism in sport. Use the information on these two pages, your own knowledge and experience, and the Internet.

3 Do you believe there are equal opportunities for girls and boys in sport? Discuss.

4 Look at Figure 1.5. What types of discrimination has Hope Powell met in her career?

5 What does the interview tell you about Hope's family and culture?

6 Look at Figure 1.6. What is Sir Alex Ferguson's opinion on racism and education?

7 Did you know there is a national campaign to rid football of racism? Have you seen posters saying 'Give racism the red card' or the magazine *Kick It Out*? Find out more from their website by visiting www.heinemann.co.uk/hotlinks.

Check it out

What you should have learned from this chapter

Look at the areas of study in the table. You should now know and understand the terminology and concepts that we have explored in Chapter 1: School.

The activities and questions in the chapter, and the worksheets your teacher will have worked through with you, should have helped you to learn about this topic.

If some of the areas are not clear, read through the pages again. If you are still not sure ask your teacher to explain them again.

You should be able to answer all the following questions. These are short answer questions similar to those that will appear in Section A of the written exam paper that you will sit at the end of the course.

The knowledge and concepts covered in this chapter will also be tested in longer, more detailed questions in Sections B and D of the exam paper.

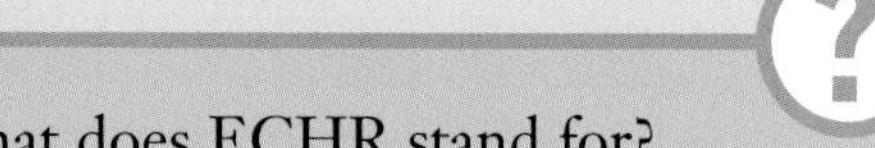

1. What does ECHR stand for?
2. How many basic human rights does the ECHR define?
3. Explain what a right is.
4. Which court safeguards these rights?
5. List six human rights.
6. What year was the Human Rights Act passed by Parliament?
7. List four responsibilities of parents.
8. Give two rights and two responsibilities of school pupils.
9. Name two organizations concerned with race relations.
10. What is the guiding principle of the Children Act of 1989?
11. Explain the term equal opportunities.
12. What is meant by charismatic authority?
13. Define coercive power.
14. Who provides the funding for schools?
15. What is a community?

2 Work

Rights and responsibilities of employers and employees

Both employers and employees have legal and moral rights and responsibilities towards one another (for a definition of legal and moral see page 9). The legal responsibilities are defined in Acts of Parliament.

Working in a factory

Recruitment

Jobs advertisements must not discriminate against you on the grounds of race, gender or age unless there are very special conditions. Recruitment and selection procedures should ensure that the most suitable person gets the job.

Major Acts that are concerned with employment

The Employment Rights Act 1996 is the main Act which covers employment law. According to this Act, everyone regardless of race, gender, age or disability has equal rights and opportunities for recruitment, pay and promotion.

The Sex Discrimination Act 1975 (see page 84), **The Race Relations Act 1976** and **The Disability Discrimination Act 1995** deal with all aspects of discrimination in recruitment and working practices.

The Equal Pay Act 1970, amended in 1984, ensures equal pay for equal work.

The National Minimum Wage Act 1998 states the minimum wage that must be paid by employers to people according to their age. (For up-to-date information contact the Minimum Wage Helpline on 0845 6000 678.)

The Factories Act 1961 and **The Health and Safety Act 1974** made employers and employees responsible for health and safety at work.

The 1992 Workplace Regulations deal with EU rules, including the safe use of computers.

The EU Working Time Directive of 1998 brought in the time limit of 48 hours for a working week.

The Trade Union and Labour Relations (Consolidation) Act 1992 and **The Trade Union Reform and Employment Rights Act 1993** determine relationships between employers and employees and trade unions.

The Employment Protection Act 1978 is concerned with redundancy, unfair dismissal and industrial tribunals.

Contracts

Once an application has been successful, the employer must supply a written document about the conditions of employment. This is often referred to as a contract.

A contract must tell the employee:

- name of the employer and employee
- job title and place(s) of work
- date of starting employment
- working hours
- rate of pay and how and when payment will be made
- holiday entitlement
- sick pay entitlement
- pension schemes if there are any
- details of complaints and disciplinary procedures
- grievance procedures
- conditions for terminating employment for both parties.

Responsibilities of an employer

An employer is responsible for:

- providing written details of the employment – a contract
- paying the wages as agreed and providing a wage slip showing the net (total) amount paid and the amounts deducted for income tax, National Insurance, etc.
- providing suitable training in health and safety at work
- providing toilets and washing facilities
- providing adequate heating, lighting and ventilation
- providing a safe place to work – this includes ensuring the safe use of all types of equipment and safe working practices, and that all workers are fully trained and follow the correct procedures
- treating employees fairly and respectfully
- allowing time off for public duties
- giving the appropriate amount of notice to terminate the employment.

Responsibilities of an employee

An employee is responsible for:

- reading, understanding and agreeing the details in the contract of employment and abiding by them (if the terms are not those agreed at interview then the employee must point this out)
- being punctual
- attending training courses on health and safety at work
- following the health and safety rules at the place of work
- carrying out all reasonable instructions in respect of the job
- ensuring their own safety and not putting anyone else at risk
- being loyal to the company and not disclosing to competing companies any information or knowledge gained by working for the company.

UK money

Your teacher will provide you with more information on wages and salaries, performance related pay and leaving a job.

Activities

1. Why is a contract of employment important to both the employer and employee?
2. Employers' responsibilities are employees' rights and vice versa. Discuss this in your group, then write down the ideas you discussed and your conclusions.

Health and safety

The HSC and HSE

Two government bodies are concerned with the health and safety of people at work.

- The Health and Safety Commission (HSC) has overall responsibility for setting policy on health and safety matters.

Activities

1. Find out who the health and safety officer is in your school. Read your school policy statement on health and safety. Discuss how it is implemented.
2. Consider the following workplaces: factories, food production lines, offices, building sites, leisure centres. What health and safety considerations would you expect in each of these?

- The Health and Safety Executive (HSE) advises on health and safety policy and enforces the health and safety laws in conjunction with all local authorities. Health and safety standards are reviewed and updated constantly to take account of new developments.

The Health and Safety Executive

The mission statement of the HSE is 'to ensure that risks to people's health and safety from work activities are properly controlled' (from the leaflet 'HSE and You' published by the HSE; more information can be found on the HSE website at www/heinemann.co.uk/hotlinks).

The HSE is concerned with ensuring that employers take full responsibility for their employees, that employees look after their own safety, and that no harm is done to members of the public due to work related activities.

The HSE enforces the law, inspecting all types of workplaces from building sites, factories and farms to schools and hospitals. Local authority officers will inspect shops, offices, hotels, etc. They give guidance and advice to people and companies of all types on the law and how the requirements can be met. They have the power to order improvements to be made and to prosecute where necessary.

Workers wearing hard hats on a building site

The Health and Safety Act 1974 gives employers and employees the responsibility to work together to ensure that the working environment is safe and healthy. Employers have to provide training in all aspects of the job from lifting heavy objects and using ladders to the use of electrical equipment, computers and visual display screens. Many companies provide employees with a staff handbook that contains the necessary information on their health and safety policy and how to report concerns.

It is the responsibility of employees to raise concerns about health or safety issues if they think a situation or working practice is dangerous or unhealthy, for example smoking in offices. An employer cannot dismiss anyone for raising concerns as long as the correct procedures are followed.

The economy

What do we mean by 'the economy'?

The economy is the way in which goods, services and finances are provided and managed. Each country has its own way of organizing its national economy. An economist will define four types of economy:

- subsistence economy – people grow their own food, gather natural resources for their own use, build houses for themselves and in general are self sufficient. There is little or no trade or production of goods and services, so people subsist. At one time this type of economy existed everywhere, so it is often known as the traditional economy. This type of economy is prevalent in Less Economically Developed Countries (LEDCs).
- market economy – consumer demand for goods and services drives the economy. The demand is satisfied by businesses mostly in private ownership or multinationals, which are totally motivated by profit. Competition between businesses ensures keen prices. This type of economy is seen mostly in the More Economically Developed Countries (MEDCs).
- planned economy – the state owns most businesses and decides what will be produced. Any businesses which do exist will be set production targets by the government which they have to meet. Consumers have little influence over the goods and services available. Most Eastern European and other former communist countries used to have this type of economy; now most have mixed economies.
- mixed economy – this is a combination of a market economy and a planned economy. Most businesses are motivated by profit and supply consumer demand for goods and services; some are multinationals. Other businesses are owned and run by the government. This type of economy is seen in many MEDCs.

The national economy

The UK has a mixed economy. Many businesses which produce a variety of goods and services for consumers make a profit for their owners and shareholders. Some businesses are owned and run by the state, for example the National Health Service. The utilities – the gas, electric, and water companies – used to be run by the government but were privatized during the 1980s and 1990s so are now run by private companies. British Rail was also privatized and different companies took over the running of various aspects of the railways. There has been some discussion about nationalizing the railways again.

The local economy

The local economy is based on the manufacturing and service industries that exist within an area or region of the country. In some parts of the country where traditional types of production and manufacturing (for example ship building, steel making, coal mining) have ceased to exist or have been dramatically reduced, it is possible to obtain government grants to set up new businesses and create new jobs to generate more prosperity for the people. These areas are known as Development Areas. In Enterprise Zones, which are often in the same region as Development Areas, large companies can qualify for a variety of grants to start up in the area, which will create work for local people. In some areas grants from the EU are available.

How do businesses use financial services?

Sources of finance

Internal sources of finance are used when extra finance is needed for a short term only. The size and type of the company will determine if raising money from internal sources is appropriate. The use of external sources of finance is based on the length of time the money is needed (see Figure 2.1).

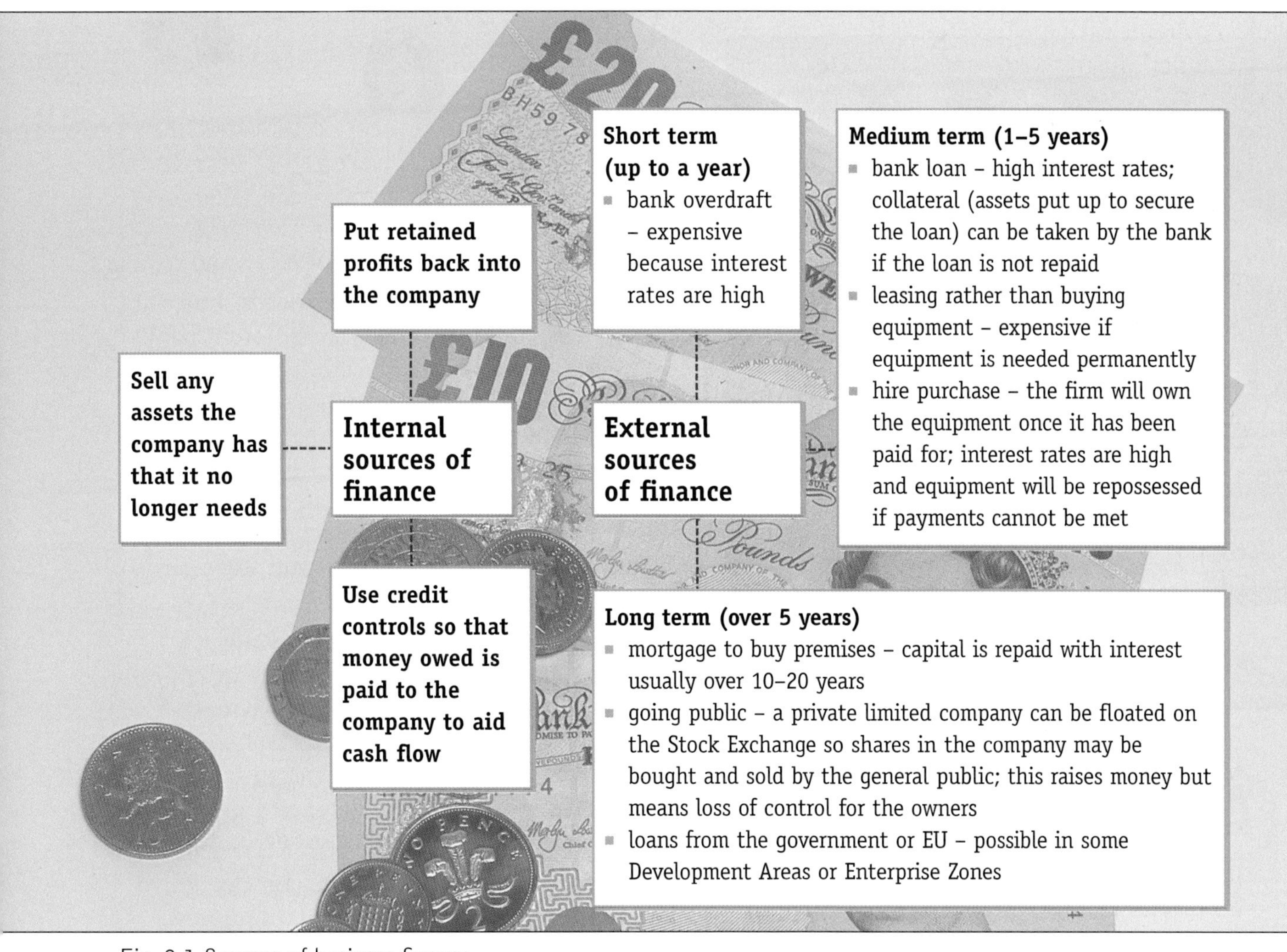

Fig. 2.1 Sources of business finance

Banks

When a small business is first set up advice may be sought from a bank's business advisor. The advisor will help with many important aspects of setting up a business and drawing up a business plan and will know the local organizations which may be able to help.

Banks offer business bank accounts and make charges for operating these accounts. Usually every transaction has a fixed charge. Phone-based banking services and some (Internet) on-line banking services are also available.

Banks will lend money to businesses as a direct loan for a fixed length of time at a rate of interest. A mortgage may be available to buy business premises. Some banks also offer special business insurance services.

Making deals in the city

Activity

Try to organize a visit from a bank manager to talk to your group about business and personal financial matters.

Money matters – you and your money

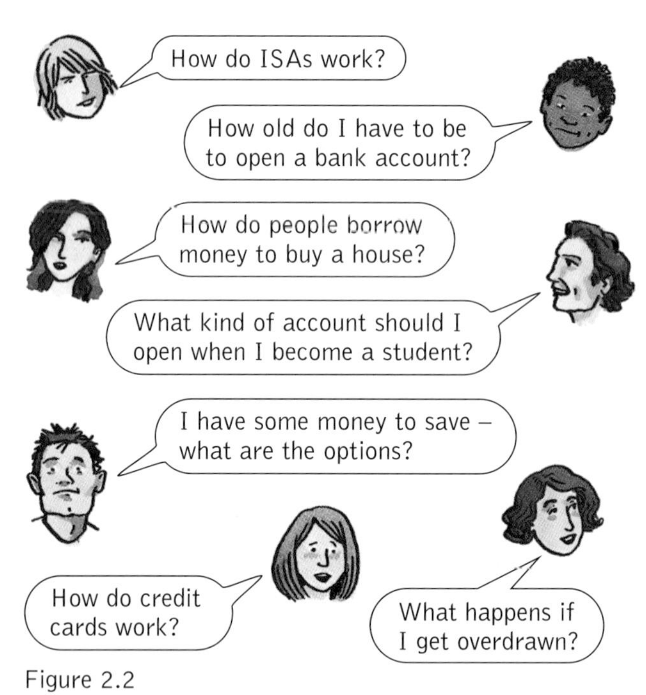

Figure 2.2

Different types of account

To get the account to suit your needs, find out as much as you can about what different banks and building societies will offer you. Frequently, special accounts are available for young people up to a certain age, and student accounts for those in further or higher education. Most people open an ordinary current account when they start earning a living. Cash cards, credit cards and store cards are also used by many people.

To save money choose between savings accounts, investment accounts or savings bonds, as well as ISAs (Individual Savings Accounts).

There are a number of ways to borrow money for something special, e.g. a car or a house. Be careful, lenders will always charge a rate of interest on the loan. Make sure you can afford to pay back the loan and the rate of interest.

Current accounts

A current account is the most common type of account. You usually have to be eighteen or over to open a current account. Money can be paid into this account directly by your employer, so you do not need to carry large amounts of cash to the bank. You don't even have to visit your bank to pay in your pay cheque. You are given a cheque book and most banks offer a cash card too. You can take money out of this account by cashing a cheque or using the cash card at an ATM (Automatic Teller Machine). On-line banking is now available through the Internet.

As you know, a cash card is a small piece of plastic which contains your own personal details. You access your cash by putting the card into the cash machine and entering your PIN (Personal Identification Number) and the amount you wish to withdraw. Never let anyone else use your cash card. Notify the bank if you lose it or it is stolen, as someone else could use it to gain access to your money.

You can also arrange an overdraft on this account. This means that you make an arrangement with the bank to lend you money up to a fixed amount for a short period of time. This is then paid back to the bank. But be careful – the rates of interest charged on the amount overdrawn can be very high. You should never write a cheque knowing that you do not have enough money in the account to cover it. This is illegal, and is known as fraud.

Using cash cards

Savings

Savings accounts vary according to the amount you want to save. You can either save a lump sum (a fixed amount) or a regular amount each month.

The amount of interest your savings earn will depend on how quickly you say you need access to your money. For example, you may have a 30 or 60 day account which means that you will need to give 30 or 60 days' notice that you wish to withdraw some of your money. The longer the notice the greater the interest.

Some accounts may allow you to withdraw up to a limited amount on demand (without notice) without losing any interest.

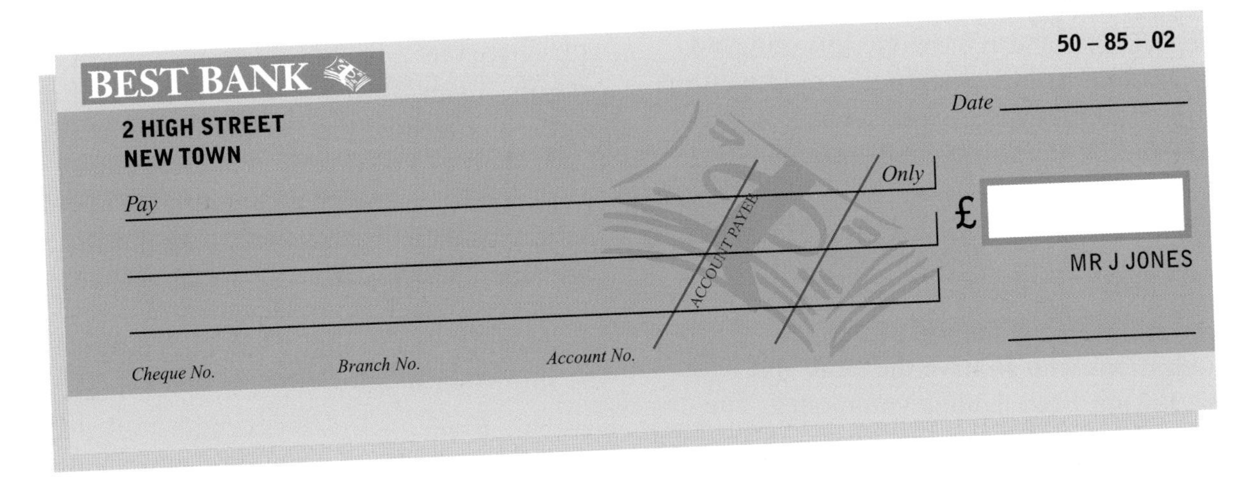

Figure 2.3 A blank cheque

Saving for that beach holiday

Other types of accounts give more interest if you agree to leave your money for a fixed term, usually a number of years – the longer the term the greater the rate of interest.

Interest is the amount of money the account gains over a period of time expressed as a percentage. Tax is usually charged on all amounts of interest.

You can arrange to save a fixed amount each month and have that paid directly into a savings account from your current account.

What is an ISA?

An ISA is an Individual Savings Account. You do not have to pay any tax on the interest your money earns. You can have one ISA only and there is a limit to the amount you can invest or save in an ISA during each tax year. It is well worth considering this type of account.

Borrowing money

Credit cards

These are issued by many financial organizations who all have the same aim – to make a profit from lending you money. The interest charged by these organizations is considerable. Most cards will have an upper limit – a definite amount you can spend using the credit card.

When you use a credit card to buy goods or services the financial organization pays the bill. At the end of each month they will send you an account which gives details of all the transactions you have made using the card, and the total amount which you owe. You now have two options – to pay the account completely and owe nothing thereby paying no interest, or to pay the minimum amount requested or more and be charged interest on the outstanding (remaining) balance. This will increase each month as you will be charged interest on the interest. Be careful – it can be very, very expensive and it is extremely easy to build up a large amount of debt in this way.

Store cards

These are similar to credit cards and are issued by most large shops. They can be used to buy goods in that shop only and work on the same principle as credit cards. They can be useful, especially if you clear the balance each month. But if you don't, it can be an extremely expensive way to purchase goods because they also charge very high interest rates.

Hire purchase

This is a type of loan where you agree to pay back the amount borrowed (the cost of the item purchased, for example washing machine, TV or car) by repaying a definite amount every month. Again, a fixed rate of interest is charged and is included within the amount to be paid back. This can be expensive – always make sure you know what the total charges are. There is a period, usually three days after signing an agreement, during which you can change your mind and cancel the arrangement. Read the documents very carefully before you sign and be sure you can afford the repayments.

Companies can repossess the goods if the payments are not made. However, some companies offer 'interest free' loans if the total amount is repaid within a certain time.

Always be very sure you understand the terms of the agreement before you sign it.

Activities

Look at these different scenarios and decide which account or method of saving would be best. Be sure you can justify your answers.

- A relative wins the lottery and gives you £1000.
- You want to save for a special holiday after your exams.
- You have a Saturday job and want to save a small amount regularly.
- You are going to College and need a bank account.

Types of business

In the UK different types of business operate in different sectors of the mixed economy.

A sole trader This business is owned and run by one person – the owner. The owner will probably employ other people, but all the control of the business is in the hands of the owner, who takes all the risks and keeps all the profits. If the business is unsuccessful, the owner would be entirely responsible for any debts. There are 3–4 million sole traders in this country.

A partnership is an agreement between two or more people to establish and run a company. There cannot be more than 20 partners in any one business. The partners provide the finance, make decisions and share all the risks and responsibilities of running the business.

A public limited company (plc) must have a board of directors who run the company, and must hold annual general meetings for its

Market day – a traditional way of doing business

shareholders. The shares are traded on the Stock Exchange and may be bought by individuals or organizations. The shareholders have limited liability, which means that they can only be held liable for debts up to the value of their shares.

A private limited company (Ltd) is usually made up of a small number of people (at least two) who buy shares in the company and thereby become part owners of the company. The shares are not traded on the Stock Exchange and can only be bought by the people who started the company. The shareholders have limited liability.

A person buys a **franchise** (franchisee) from a well-known and established company to run a business along specific guidelines set out by the franchisor. The franchisee pays the franchisor a percentage of the annual profits, known as a royalty.

In a **co-operative** all the workers buy shares in the business and it is therefore owned by all the workers. Everyone is involved in the finance and decision-making of the company.

Industry sectors

All businesses are in trade to make a profit. They provide services or manufacture products. All production is divided into one of the following sectors.

- The primary sector extracts raw materials and natural resources from the ground or sea by mining, quarrying or fishing. It also includes farming. Animals are classed as a natural resource for these purposes so farmers who breed animals for slaughter are included in this sector.
- The secondary sector uses the raw materials and natural resources gathered or grown by the primary sector and makes (manufactures) them into a completed product, for example frozen pizza, cars, houses.
- The tertiary sector is the service sector. A service may be provided to industry such as advertising or distribution of goods, or to consumers such as shops and supermarkets, pubs or leisure centres. Services such as education, the police, fire service and the National Health Service are also included in this sector.
- The quaternary sector is also a service sector, but a specialized sector developed as a result of the technological advances made during the last few years. This sector involves telecommunications and the Internet in the provision of services such as call centres and on-line banking and shopping.

Activity

Create a chart to show the different types of production giving local and national examples of each type. List as many different examples as you can.

A busy call centre

Case study: Nissan Motor Manufacturing (UK) Ltd

The company

Japan is the home of Nissan, a multinational car manufacturing company. In 1984 Nissan chose an airfield in Sunderland in the north-east of England as the site for establishing its centre of production for passenger cars in Europe. This brought much needed investment into the region as the traditional industries of ship building, steel production and coal mining were declining.

The site was chosen because:

- it was a large area (300 hectares) of flat land that could easily be built on
- there were very good road and rail links to all parts of the country and two sea ports were nearby
- the local people and trade unions had positive attitudes
- the area had an excellent name for engineering
- the site was in an Enterprise Zone and a grant of £100 million was available.

The company has invested over £1.5 billion in the site. The production of cars began in 1986. Between 1986 and 2002 more than 2 million cars were made in Sunderland. Of these, 1.4 million were exported to 58 different countries.

This investment in the area by Nissan Motor Manufacturing (UK) Ltd has led to the creation of 5000 jobs within the car plant itself and another 10 000 jobs within the area as component suppliers have expanded to manufacture parts to supply the car plant.

The employees

Staff recruitment and selection procedures are very rigorous. Applicants have to complete a range of tests, practical exercises and interviews successfully before being offered a job. In 1999, 800 new staff were appointed out of 11 000 applicants.

While the site was being developed in 1985 Nissan negotiated a single union deal for the plant with the AEU (Amalgamated Engineering Union). There have not been any industrial disputes and no production time has been lost. As part of the agreement with the AEU a company council was set up. Employees are elected, by secret ballot, to serve as members of council for a term of four years. This has been very successful in maintaining good relationships between the company, the employees and the union. The company council discusses company business and negotiates salaries, and terms and conditions of employment.

Nissan operates a 'Single Policy Status', which means that all employees have equal opportunity, the same terms and conditions of employment, and enjoy the same company benefits. Workers are monitored and informed about their performance. Targets are set and reviewed annually.

The Nissan factory in Sunderland

Kaizen is a Japanese word meaning continuous improvement. The kaizen process is operated at Nissan. This means ideas and suggestions for improvements can be made, discussed, tried out, then modified and finally put into operation as the standard for that part of the manufacturing process.

Health and safety

The health and safety section within the company deals with safety (from the design stage onwards), occupational health, occupational hygiene, fire prevention, and health and safety training. Health and safety is essential and everyone has their part to play. All new employees go through health and safety training as part of their induction process (introduction to the company). In the design of the car assembly line and the manufacturing equipment, health and safety issues are very important factors.

Car production

The production of cars at Nissan revolves around the JIT (Just In Time) principle. This means 'using the minimum amount of resources in the most efficient way'. It involves frequent deliveries of relatively small batches of components so that the Nissan plant does not have to store, move or check the quality of the components. Nissan has established supplier development teams to guarantee that products of the required quality are always delivered on time.

The result is more cost effective because the system reduces the need to buy in bulk, therefore less capital (money) is needed to pay for stored goods. Fewer people are needed to move and handle car parts and the quality controls are operated by the supplier, again reducing labour costs.

Employees work in teams with a supervisor who will monitor the quality and speed of their work. Each employee is able to cover three jobs within an area. This allows flexibility as one employee can cover three jobs, while each job can be done by three people. Jobs and skills are rotated at regular intervals.

Robots

Over 250 robots are used on the production line. Most robots are used in the body shop where repetitive tasks such as spot welding and sealing inner and outer panels are done. Robots are used in the paint shop to apply undercoat and sealers and in the final assembly shop to seal light clusters and windscreens.

Robots are used because they can work in areas that are unsuitable for people, remove the boredom of repetitive jobs and produce a finish that is of consistent quality and accuracy.

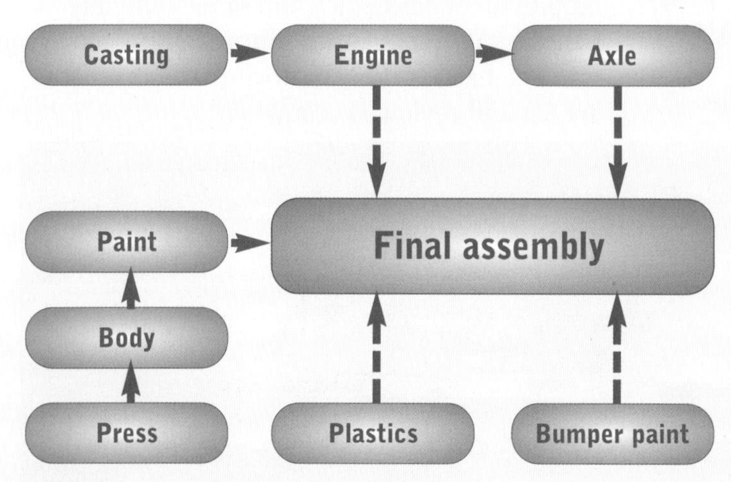

Figure 2.3 Car production at Nissan

Environmentally friendly?

With any large-scale manufacturing plant pollution is a danger to the environment. Nissan take great care to do as much as possible for the local environment. Noise from the press plant is reduced to the minimum and the plant is said to be one of the quietest in Europe. Waste liquids, especially from the paint shop, are filtered and heavy metals are removed up to 10 per cent below the legal limits.

The suppliers use returnable packaging and components are delivered by being transported collectively. This means the components are collected from each supplier and delivered all together rather than being delivered separately from all over Europe. This is thought to reduce the transport distance by about 100 million kilometres and to save 32 million litres of fuel.

Forty hectares of the original site have been retained as environmental areas for wildlife. There is a reservoir for wildfowl and a wildflower meadow has been created to encourage wildlife.

The local economy

The opening of the Nissan Motor Manufacturing plant in Sunderland has done much to stimulate the local and regional economy and increase prosperity for the north-east of England.

Many companies within the region now supply components to Nissan. Over 200 companies from around the UK and Europe supply goods worth more than £1 billion to the Nissan plant each year. Some of the suppliers have located their businesses near to the Nissan plant. Nissan believe that 'Sunderland is now the UK's fastest growing automotive manufacturing centre'.

It has been estimated that Nissan contributes around £400 million annually to the local economy. This is a much needed boost to the local and regional economy, which has seen a decline in the traditional manufacturing industries.

Nissan Motor Manufacturing (UK) has developed partnerships with schools – 2500 pupils visit the plant every year. Local suppliers and community groups are also taken on guided tours. Employees are actively involved in raising funds for the charity NCH Action for Children. The company has sponsored well-known sporting events such as a series of The Great North Run and the Yellow Brick Road Rally to raise funds for a hospice.

A Nissan car, made in Sunderland

A Nissan car being put together on the factory floor

The national economy

The Enterprise Zones that were created in the mid-1980s were designed to promote the economic growth of certain areas around the country. The government invested in grants to companies which established businesses in these zones. A grant of £100 million was given to Nissan. However, since then Nissan has invested over £1.5 billion in the Sunderland car plant, creating over 15 000 permanent jobs (in a region where unemployment is still high) and generating millions of pounds for the local and therefore national economy.

This development has created extra trade and growth in exports (of cars) and a flourishing industry in the supply of components. This has increased local prosperity, and benefited the national economy.

Activities

1. What level of production is carried out at Nissan – primary, secondary, tertiary or quaternary? Explain your answer.
2. In what ways does the company operate equality of opportunity for employees?
3. Describe Nissan's health and safely policy.
4. What contribution has Nissan made to the local economy?
5. Explain the JIT principle.
6. Is the Sunderland plant environmentally friendly? Explain your answer.
7. In your opinion, is Nissan helping the local and regional economy to prosper? How?

What's your opinion of work experience?

Its just working for nothing.

Work experience is a week off school.

?

I'm looking forward to doing something different for a change.

It's a great opportunity.

Figure 2.4

Learning new skills on work experience

The success of your work experience placement really does depend on your approach to it. If you are interested, show that you are willing to learn, are polite and ask sensible questions, you will gain a great deal. Use the time wisely: discover more about the company and the people – then you will probably enjoy it *and* be a good ambassador for your school.

If you are presenting work experience as your assessed coursework component of the examination, you must make sure that you include evidence for all the sections of the mark scheme.

Your teacher will guide you through this and there is more help in Section 4 which is all about coursework and the exam.

Activities

Produce a case study of a company of your choice.

1 Find out about:

- the type of company (partnership, limited company, etc.)
- recruitment and job descriptions
- equal opportunities
- health and safety policy
- links with other businesses
- contribution to the local, regional and national economy.

2 Use your ICT skills to include:

- graph(s) and chart(s)
- a photograph or picture of the company
- a picture or drawing of the product the company makes, if it is a manufacturing business
- a map to show the location of the business.

Check it out

What you should have learned from this section

Look at the areas of study in the table. You should now know and understand the terminology and concepts that we have explored in Chapter 2: Work.

The activities and questions in the chapter, and the extra sheets your teacher will have worked through with you, should have helped you to learn about this topic.

If some of the areas are not clear, read through the pages again. If you are still not sure, ask your teacher to explain them again.

Area of study	Page
The laws affecting employment	29
The rights and responsibilities of employers and employees	29
Contracts of employment – salaries, redundancy and unfair dismissal	30
Health and safety at work	31
The economy and business finance	32
Your money	34
Business and industry – types of business and industry sectors	37

You should be able to answer all the following questions. These are short answer questions similar to those that will appear in Section A of the written exam paper that you will sit at the end of the course.

The knowledge and concepts covered in this chapter will also be tested in longer, more detailed questions in Section B and D of the exam paper.

?

1. Name three Acts of Parliament which are concerned with employment.
2. What is a contract of employment?
3. List three responsibilities of an employer.
4. What does HSC stand for?
5. Why is the Health and Safety Act important?
6. Explain the difference between a credit card and a store card.
7. What is a plc? Give an example.
8. List three different types of production and give examples of each one.
9. Explain the term a mixed economy.
10. Give two ways a company could raise extra finance.

3 Local community

Community life

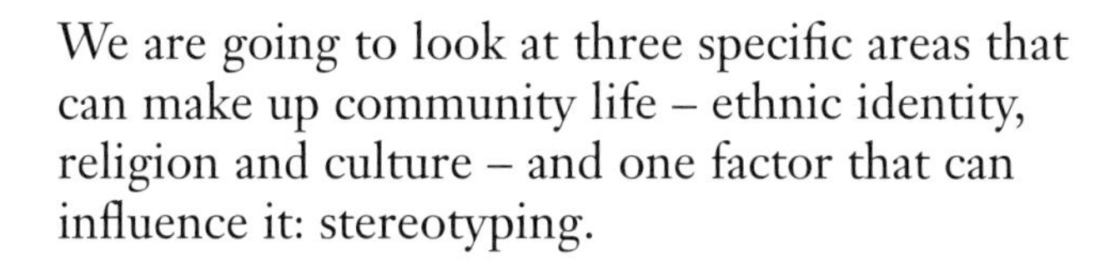

We are going to look at three specific areas that can make up community life – ethnic identity, religion and culture – and one factor that can influence it: stereotyping.

Stereotypes

A stereotype is where we have a *fixed* idea of who, or what, someone or something is. People often stereotype ethnic groups, a religion, or a culture. These fixed ideas can affect community life.

Ethnic identity

The term ethnic identity or ethnicity is often used to refer to minority groups within a society. Ethnic identity refers to a particular way of life or culture (language, lifestyle, customs) of a group within a society or community.

When people of different ethnic identities live in a community the culture of that community is much more varied. Sometimes this can cause problems if one ethnic group feels it is being treated unfairly or being victimized. When this happens it is usually headline news, as reported in 2001 in cities such as Bradford (your teacher will give you a sheet about this topic).

Activities

1. Discuss how far your opinions about a cultural, ethnic or religious group are based on stereotypes.
2. Stereotypes of any ethnic, religious or cultural group are usually inaccurate and misleading – why?

Ethnic identity takes many forms ...

Religion

Religion is a general term which means a system of belief in a particular faith, set of values, practices, rites and worship – often of an invisible supernatural power or being.

Members of a particular religion will be expected to conform to a defined set of beliefs and practices. This will affect their attitudes and behaviour and may lead to:

- social cohesion – the followers of the religion have a common belief and set of values. They usually meet together to worship regularly and will support each other during times of stress, for example illness or the death of a loved one. This creates a sense of belonging and worth in a community.

Who worships here?

- social control – the religion will provide very clear rules of behaviour and specify consequences if the expected behaviour code is not followed, thereby controlling behaviour patterns throughout life.

A local place of worship can be a point of social contact as well as a place of spiritual worship. A number of social activities may be organized by members of the religious community which benefit the whole community, for example a toddler group or playgroup for pre-school children, after-school clubs, a youth club. Many people in the community will use these facilities without being members of the religious community.

Religion can sometimes cause strife in a community if followers of different religions do not tolerate each other's beliefs. This can result in tension and conflict which may erupt into violence and adversely affect normal peaceful community life.

Activities

1. How many different religions can you think of?
2. Make a list or an ideas web of all the different religions your group can think of.
3. Discuss where these different religions came from and what their beliefs are.
4. Discuss which different religions are practised in your community.
5. What conflicts can you think of that have been caused by religion? Use the Internet to find information on the current state of the conflicts. Have any of the conflicts been resolved? If so, how?

Culture

The term culture means the shared language, behaviours, customs, traditions and values of a society. The values in a society refer to things that people believe are important and worthwhile. Values will change over time even within the same society or group, but these changes do not happen quickly. The values different ethnic groups have will vary too. The way in which the culture patterns are learned is by the process of socialization.

Ethnic groups will have their own distinct traditions, customs and values which may be similar to, or very distinct from, the culture of the majority of the community.

Community life can be enriched for all people within a community if everyone is willing to accept each other's culture and live peacefully as neighbours through mutual co-operation and understanding.

Community life can be adversely affected by clashes of different cultures when people are unwilling to understand others. Some then become fearful of the unknown and intolerant, which leads to misunderstanding and tension. In turn this can develop into disturbances which disrupt the normal harmony of community life.

Activities

1 Compare and contrast two different cultures – your own culture and one other of your choice. How would you describe the following with regard to each culture?
   - type of family
   - marriage
   - how children are brought up
   - how children are educated
   - fashions and dress code
   - popular music
   - food, diet and eating patterns
   - religion
   - festivals celebrated.

2 Different groups within the same society, for example teenagers, may have slightly different behaviour and values from the wider culture they belong to. Think about this in a small group and identify the differences in a teenage culture.

Notting Hill Carnival

Local government

Local government systems

There are normally two tiers of local government:

- Town, city, district and county councils and unitary authorities meet in town or city halls, district council offices, civic centres or shire halls. Councillors serve a term of four years. They are responsible for council housing, education, police and fire services, paving and street lighting, roads, libraries, arts, leisure and sports, and social services. Councils are funded from the council tax and from taxes raised by the national government.

Local councillors in council chambers

- Parish councils are locally elected within a parish area. Parish councillors are elected to serve a maximum of four years. They are responsible for local services: village halls, playing fields and rights of way. Their funding comes from a small part of the council tax.

A new constitution for local authorities

In 2000 the government informed all local authorities in the country that they must set up a new constitution. They offered three options for consideration:

- a leader with a cabinet of councillors (see Figure 3.1)
- a directly elected mayor with a cabinet of councillors
- a directly elected mayor with a council manager.

Local authorities consulted people, organizations and businesses about their preferred option for their area. Some local authorities arranged a referendum so the people on the register of electors for the area could vote for their chosen option. All local authorities are required to ensure that their decisions are closely scrutinized and monitored.

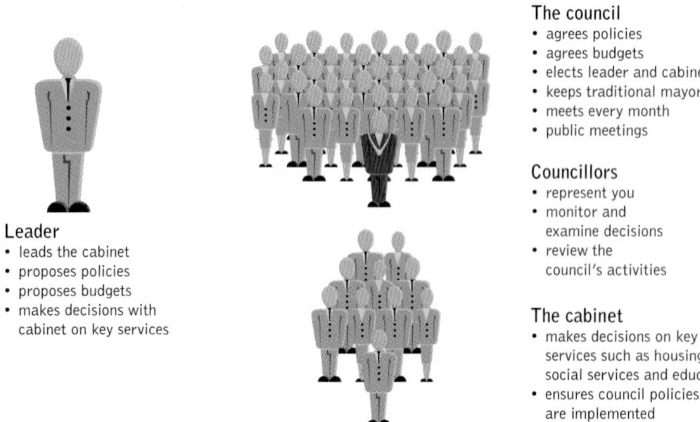

Figure 3.1 A leader with a cabinet of councillors
This is based on the proposed system at Gateshead Council

Financing local services

A local council raises finance through the council tax and also receives finance from central government for development and specific projects, for example meeting the costs of national pay awards.

The local council spends money according to the council policy on education, social services, leisure, housing, libraries, cleansing, community events, repairs, roads, lighting, parks and environmental issues. The amount of money the council chooses to spend on each of these areas of responsibility can affect the quality of people's lives on a daily basis.

It is important to choose the party who represents your views when the time comes to elect your representative on the council, or you may find that local conditions change and that your needs are not met.

If you feel that the council is not taking your needs into account you can arrange to meet your local councillor, or go to a surgery which your local councillors hold regularly, and express your views. Our local environment and services are crucial to the quality of our everyday living and the standard of the services provided are determined by the local councillors and the council staff.

Council workers

Activities

1. Find out what system of government your area has at local level. How was the decision to choose this option made?
2. Find out where your local council meets.
3. What are the names of your local councillors? Which political party, if any, do they represent?
4. Find out the names of the leader of your local council and the person responsible for education policy on the council.
5. How does your local council keep you informed about what is happening in your area? Do you think this is enough?
6. Try to attend a council meeting to note how decisions about your area are made.
7. Name the departments in your local council.

Devolution – regional government in the UK

Devolution is the transfer or delegation of power to a lower level, especially from central government to local or national administrations. For centuries, Britain has been governed by a central government. Now there is a Scottish Parliament and assemblies in Northern Ireland and Wales (Figure 3.2). Some people think that there should be an English Parliament to look after the issues relating to England. Other people believe that a central government does not understand the needs of regions within England, so there should be regional government.

Activities

1. There should be a system of regional government in England. Discuss.
2. Find the names and political parties of the first ministers of Scotland, Northern Ireland and Wales using the Internet.
3. Do you think that some regional governments should have the right to raise taxes while others don't?

	Scottish Parliament	Welsh Assembly	Northern Ireland Assembly
Meets in	Edinburgh	Cardiff	Belfast
Number of members	129	60	108 (executive is made up of representatives of all main political parties)
Method of election	**Additional member system** 73 represent single-member constituencies, 56 elected from regional lists supplied by political parties	**Additional member system** 4 represent single-member constituencies, 20 elected from regional lists	**Single transferable vote**
Powers	• Can increase taxes for Scotland beyond national tax level and use revenue in Scotland • Makes decisions about issues relating to regional affairs, education and health spending • Makes new laws for Scotland – as a result is responsible for home affairs in Scotland	• No tax raising powers • Cannot make separate laws for Wales • Makes decisions regarding regional affairs, education, health authorities, local government	• Makes decisions regarding education, health and local government • Takes the lead in economic development • Required by Good Friday Agreement of 1998 to participate in talks with Irish Republic about common issues such as transport and agriculture

Figure 3.2

Voting systems

Many people argue that the present system that Britain uses to determine the national government is not truly representative of how people vote in elections. In 1997, using the first past the post system, the Labour Party took 418 seats in Parliament (63 per cent) with 43.2 per cent of the vote. The Conservative Party failed to have a representative from Wales or Scotland in the 1997 election despite winning 19.6 per cent and 17.5 per cent respectively of the votes cast. The Electoral Reform Society and other pressure groups would argue that Labour voters are over-represented and Conservative voters are under-represented in Parliament through the first past the post system and that reform is long overdue.

After the 1997 general election the government set up a commission, headed by Lord Jenkins, to look at electoral reform. The Jenkins Commission examined different voting systems, particularly those that are proportional but that keep a link between MPs and their constituents. The Jenkins Commission Report, which was published in October 1998, recommended that a system called AV plus should be introduced. This is the Alternative Vote System with a top-up element. It would allow 15–20 per cent of MPs to be selected on a citywide, district or county basis. A referendum is proposed to ask people if they would like to change to the new system.

Activities

1. Which system of proportional representation do you consider to be the fairest and why? Can you see any disadvantages to some of the systems?
2. Any election system should produce a clear result. How clear are the results from the electoral systems described here?
3. Should there be a regional government in your area, for example a North-East Assembly? Discuss.

Voting systems

Single Transferable Vote – used to elect members of local, regional and European government in Northern Ireland. The number of constituencies is reduced so that each constituency has a greater number of MPs. Voters are required to select candidates in order of preference by placing numbers in descending order against names. The amount of votes a candidate requires to win the seat is determined by the size of the seat. Surplus votes are transferred to other candidates.

Additional Member System – used for elections to the Scottish Parliament and the Welsh Assembly. Half the members are elected using the first past the post system. The other half are selected according to the percentage of votes cast for each party from a list of party nominees in priority order.

Alternative Vote System (AVS) elects one MP. Voters place numbers against the names of all the candidates in priority order. Candidates must have more than 50 per cent of the votes cast to win. If no candidate achieves this an exhaustive ballot is held. This removes the candidate with the lowest vote and then counts the voters' second choice and adds it to the other candidates' totals. This continues until only one candidate remains.

Regional List System – used for elections to the European Parliament. The system requires voters to select a party rather than a candidate. The country is divided into regions electing several MPs. The parties are allocated the number of seats which corresponds with their share of the vote.

National List System – used in Italy and Israel. Voters vote for a party and the proportion of votes cast for each party determines the proportion of seats the party will have in government.

How individuals can bring about change

Political parties

A political party is a collection of individuals who meet at local, regional and national level with other individuals who share the same political views. They form national parties to maximize their chances of winning power at election time by pooling resources and ideas. At election time each political party produces a manifesto which sets out the type of action the party will take if it is elected to form the government at local or national level.

The three main political parties in Britain are the Conservative Party, the Labour Party and the Liberal Democrats. In Wales and Scotland there are active national parties called the Scottish Nationalist Party and Plaid Cymru. In Northern Ireland the political parties are split into three distinct camps – the Unionist parties, the Social Democratic Labour Party and Sinn Fein.

The Green Party campaigning

Smaller parties include the Green Party, the National Front, the Socialist Party and the UK Independence Party. These smaller parties tend to focus on specific issues rather than the broad spectrum of issues encompassed by the policies of the main parties.

Political parties produce policies at meetings and conferences and they hope to change society by gaining power at elections. In opposition, Members of Parliament (MPs) can still have their views heard by making speeches in the House of Commons. In the same way, opposition local councillors can express their views at local council level.

Voluntary organizations

Voluntary organizations are groups of people who:

- raise awareness of the conditions under which some people live
- raise money to help make the situation better
- create activities and opportunities for members of the local community to meet and share common experiences
- create opportunities for young people
- undertake work in the community to support others.

Many voluntary organizations are charities. While the charity has paid officers who undertake leadership and administrative functions, the work of raising and collecting money is often undertaken by locally organized groups of individuals who work voluntarily.

National organizations such as Childline raise public awareness of the problems facing children. People then choose to support the work of the organization by donating money and time to its activities. Childline becomes a voice for children and its views are sought and considered at national level.

A 'Fun run' for charity

At international level the work of charities, such as Oxfam, Save the Children and the Red Cross, is crucial to the management of disaster and the development of social and technical systems in other countries.

Charities work to raise awareness and change attitudes and conditions, for example in early 2002 the Red Cross were active in striving to have the first prisoners from Afghanistan designated as prisoners of war to ensure that they were given fair treatment.

At local level voluntary organizations may be connected to religious communities, the local council or community centres. They include youth groups like the Guides and Scouts, sporting clubs, senior citizen and housebound groups and groups to support carers. They are active in the local community and if funding or conditions change to the point where a group is jeopardized, they would lobby locally. A list of the voluntary organizations in your area is available from your local council.

Pressure groups

A pressure group is a collection of people who aim to influence or change government policy. Pressure groups usually focus on one issue or area of government policy, which will often have an impact at local as well as national level. They are well organized and usually have aims and objectives which they can explain to the general public to generate support. They will have a group headquarters, membership with fees and, probably, a web page. There are a wide range of pressure groups in Britain including:

- those representing employers, for example the Confederation of British Industry
- those representing employees, for example trade unions and professional associations
- those promoting a cause or issue, for example the Campaign for Nuclear Disarmament
- those wishing to influence an area of government policy, for example the Countryside Alliance.
- those challenging international injustices, for example, Amnesty International campaign against child soldiering.

Some organizations work to promote issues on an international scale and relate to national and European government and the United Nations.

Amnesty International is campaigning against child soldiers in Uganda

These organizations include Greenpeace, Amnesty International and the Red Cross. Some pressure groups are very successful because the public agrees with their cause and joins the organization. This may be why some pressure groups have a growing membership while membership of political parties is in decline.

Supporters of pressure groups have argued that they are more effective than political parties. Pressure groups seek to influence events and decision-making in their sphere of interest. This could be in areas such as the environment, human rights, the countryside, employment law, education, discrimination, health and disability rights.

Activities

1 Which pressure group would you join, and why? Make a record of the top five pressure groups chosen by your group.

2 Contact your local council and ask for the list of voluntary organizations in your area. Vote for the organization you are most interested in and arrange for a representative to come and talk to your group about its work.

3 If you were to join a political party, which one would it be and why?

4 Find out if there are any focus groups in your community. What problem are they focusing on?

Focus groups

A focus group is a collection of individuals, often with different backgrounds and political beliefs, who join together because of a common focus. The groups usually focus on issues that relate to the local community such as school closures, incorrect use of a local incinerator or the redesignation of local land use. Focus groups meet until the problem they are facing has been resolved. They often take advice from national bodies and some have been known to challenge decisions in court.

A focus group protests against cuts in education

Formal consultation

When the government wants to build a new road or undertake a new building project on brown or green belt land, then local councils are informed. The plans are made available to members of the public and public meetings are held. The public meeting schedule and agenda is published so members of the public know where and when the meetings will be held. The public's views and opinions are heard at these meetings, though it is also possible to put agreement or opposition to a plan in writing. Strong public opposition to a proposal can lead to plans being amended or dropped.

If the government feels it is necessary, it will call a public inquiry into a problem. These are very formal proceedings. Members of the public usually organize themselves into a focus group and arrange to be represented at the inquiry. The inquiry chairperson will produce a report of the inquiry findings and present them to the government for consideration and possible legislation.

Trade unions

One example of a sectional pressure group is the trade union. It is a special example of a pressure group in that it is a collection of workers who are connected through a particular job or trade and who have joined as a group to promote their common interests.

Membership of a union does not depend on age, race, gender, political persuasion, religious belief or social status. However, the trade union movement in the form of the Trades Union Congress (TUC) has been linked with the Labour movement and the Labour Party throughout its history. This has afforded the TUC an influence in the policy-making of British governments. In addition, trade unions have used the full range of techniques available to other pressure groups to raise awareness of their aims and concerns. However, as a group, trade unions have one power that is unavailable to other pressure groups – the power of striking or working to rule. Striking means that a worker stops working until the union demands are met. Working to rule means that workers refuse to do any work other than that for which they are contracted until negotiations are completed satisfactorily.

Trade unions supporting Post Office workers in recent strikes

Trade unions hold routine meetings with employers to promote health and safety issues, to discuss pay and conditions of service and develop the industry to everyone's benefit. They also represent workers in court cases which may end in improved working conditions for individuals. This legal work has acted as a precedent for other reforms and legislation.

Lobbyists

The term lobby has come to mean the way a person or group tries to influence a government decision. This is because MPs meet people who come to talk to them in the central lobby of the Houses of Parliament. Lobbyists meet individuals or groups of MPs and persuade them to take up their cause. This means asking questions in the House of Commons and raising issues at committee meetings.

A lobbyist is usually a professional person who is employed to try to influence or change government decisions. Lobbyists are employed by a range of groups including trade unions, companies, pressure groups and charities. Lobbyists help their clients by:

- telling them who is the most appropriate person to approach
- arranging meetings between MPs, ministers and clients
- presenting strategies which could influence decisions
- preparing a timetable for the lobby and arranging media coverage.

Protests

The now historical Campaign for Nuclear Disarmament (CND), marching in 1958

Peaceful protest has a long legal history in Britain. There have been many protests throughout British history which have raised public awareness of issues. These protests usually take the form of marches with banners and placards. An alternative method is to deliver a petition to government. Major protests have raised awareness of the issues of votes for women, unemployment, nuclear disarmament, pensions, war, fuel costs and disability rights among others. The government usually takes the views of peaceful protesters into account when formulating debates in Parliament or undertaking policy reviews.

Environmentalists, protesting to save our trees

Keeping pressure lawful

Pressure groups must choose the techniques by which they hope to influence public and government opinion carefully. Sometimes they will commission a public opinion survey to be organized by MORI or some other firm to test public opinion and strength of feeling towards an issue. Sometimes they will use the media to argue their point of view or place an advertisement. Sometimes they will promote a specific cause on a particular day or week, for example National No Smoking Day, which is usually one Wednesday in March.

Unlawful pressure is applied when a person creates civil disobedience by breaking the law using non-violent means. For example the environmentalist, Swampy, broke the law in a dispute about a second runway at Manchester Airport by occupying land without permission. Very few pressure groups resort to violent protest, though the Animal Liberation Group has attacked property where experiments take place.

Activities

1. Do you think that trade unions continue to provide a useful service in modern Britain today? Give reasons for your answer.
2. Find out if your local council is consulting the public over plans at present and try to attend a meeting.
3. List five issues which you consider should be the subject for a protest. Explain why you have chosen the five.

UNIVERSITY COLLEGE WORCESTER LIBRARY

Case study: Making changes

For a number of years people who worked part time or had fixed term contracts did not have the same rights and entitlements as full-time workers. This led to many disputes and much inequality. People who had full-time jobs had many more days holiday. Annual days leave included bank holidays in some companies, but not in others. There was great variation and no minimum entitlement. Something had to be done so that part-time workers or people on short term or fixed term contracts were treated the same.

All the trade unions campaigned for equality for all workers. It is only within the last four years that this has been brought about. This has been done in two main ways:

- The Working Time Regulations 1998 limited the length of the working day and week, and gave all workers the right to at least four weeks' paid holiday after thirteen weeks of employment.
- The Part Time Workers' Regulations 2000 gave all part-time workers the same entitlements as full-time workers.

The great holiday hijack

Some Bosses are still opposing paid holidays three years after the law changed, says Neasa MacErlean.

If someone asked you to name the biggest cause of disputes over employment rights, you might say the minimum wage, long hours, maternity benefit or pensions. Yet employment advisers dealing with the public agree that holidays cause most hassles.

'It's easily the biggest single employment issue that Citizens Advice Bureaux deal with right across the country,' says Richard Dunstan of the National Association of Citizens Advice Bureaux (Nacab), which together deal with 600,000 employment queries a year. Richard says that many people at the low-paid end of the workforce are losing out. 'Many people aren't getting paid holiday at all, or less than the four weeks. This issue tends to go along with long hours and poor conditions.'

The Low Pay Unit says a third of the calls it receives are to do with time off.

'It generates an enormous number of phone calls,' says Sarah Veale of the TUC, which gives out free leaflets on employment issues to callers to its free information line.

At Acas, The Advisory Conciliation and Arbitration Service, too, there is continuing demand for advice.

Figure 3.3 Adapted from an article in the *Observer*, 24 February 2002.

Activities

1. Why was it necessary to make changes to holiday entitlements?
2. Who campaigned for change?
3. Have the changes brought improvements? Find out more about one trade union and how it has acted as a pressure group to bring about a change which has benefited its members.
4. What is The Low Pay Unit, and what does it do? You could look on their website at www.heinemann.co.uk/hotlinks to find out more.

Check it out

What you should have learned from this chapter

Look at the areas of study in the table. You should now know and understand the terminology and concepts that we have explored in Chapter 3: Local community.

The activities and questions in the chapter, and the extra sheets your teacher will have worked through with you, should have helped you to learn about this topic.

If some of the areas are not clear, read through the pages again. If you are still not sure, ask your teacher to explain them again.

Area of study	Page
How ethnic identity, religion and culture can affect community life	45
How local councils work	48
Regional government and devolution	50
The Scottish Parliament	50
The Welsh Assembly	50
The Northern Ireland Assembly	50
Political parties	52
Voluntary organizations	52
Pressure groups	53
Trade unions	55

You should be able to answer all the following questions. These are short answer questions similar to those that will appear in Section A of the written exam paper that you will sit at the end of the course.

The knowledge and concepts covered in this chapter will also be tested in longer, more detailed questions in Section B and D of the exam paper.

?

1. Explain what you understand by the terms:
   - ethnic identity
   - religion
   - culture.
2. Describe the three ways a local council could be organized.
3. What is devolution?
4. Name the three devolved powers and state where they are based.
5. What voting system do we use to elect Members of Parliament?
6. Name three pressure groups.
7. Choose one pressure group and give an example of how it has influenced an issue.
8. What does TUC stand for?
9. List four political parties.
10. Name a voluntary organization and state what it does.

National and European citizenship

Key ideas

Chapter 4 National and European government

* Systems of government
* The democratic system in the UK
* How national government works
* The European Union
* Taking part in the democratic process
* How national government manages the economy
* Becoming a European citizen

Chapter 5 Criminal and civil law

* How does the law affect you?
* Consumers and the law
* Young people and employment
* The law and discrimination
* What is crime?
* Law-making in action
* European laws
* I'll see you in court!

Chapter 6 The media

* How much does the media influence our lives?
* Freedom of speech
* Who controls the media?
* How is the media monitored?
* How is advertising regulated
* Are we influenced by advertising?

What about the Chinese government directed massacre at Tiananmen Square? Who were the criminals here – the protesters or the government?

What is crime? Most people agree that the murder of Stephen Lawrence was a racially motivated crime (these are the five suspects after their acquittal). Can an acquitted person ever be brought to trial again for the same crime?

How important is voting to you? Do you think voting makes a difference to our quality of life?

Do you believe everything you read, see and hear in the media?

4 National and European government

Systems of government

Different systems of government are in operation across the world.

Systems of government

Republics are led by governments and have no monarch.

One-party states have only one political party.

Constitutional monarchies are governed by a group of people elected from a range of political parties and have a monarch as head of state.

Dictatorships are ruled by one person who has authority in all matters.

Most of the countries in the world including the United Kingdom are democracies. This means that they have a free and fair voting system, freedom of speech and a choice of political parties at elections.

The word democracy comes from two Greek words meaning 'people power'. Athens is regarded as the birthplace of democracy as it held a 'people's assembly' where everyone had the right to speak. This was a system of direct democracy. In today's world there are too many people to make decisions in this way. Direct democracy is still used when a government wishes to have a decision on a major issue. This usually takes the form of a referendum.

The United Kingdom is a constitutional monarchy. The Queen is the head of state but the power of government is invested in Parliament.

The Queen at the State opening of parliament

Activities

1. In groups, discuss how you would choose to set up a new school council. Should it be direct democracy, or should it be a representative democracy like Parliament?
2. The original 'people's assembly' only allowed men to talk. Women, children, foreigners and slaves were not allowed to vote. In groups discuss what you consider to be the fairest system of government and how it can represent all sections of society.

The democratic system in the UK

A democracy is built up over time on tradition and convention. Through a country's constitution a democracy hopes to promote debate, participation and ownership of the ideals on which a country is based.

Coming of age in the UK democracy

The electoral process in the UK allows people over the age of eighteen, whose names appear on the register of electors, to vote in elections to select their representatives at local, national and European level. Sometimes the candidates are not members of political parties, and are therefore 'independent'. Mostly, candidates are connected to a political party, whose finance for election campaigns comes from its membership fees and donations from supporters.

Elections

A writ calling an election is served and nominations for candidates for the election are invited by the closing date. Candidates embark

Political party – is an organized group of people with similar views and beliefs, who have a written constitution and manifesto on which they fight an election.

Candidate – is someone who has been nominated to run for election as your representative in your political party. Candidates must be over the age of 21.

Election campaign – is the set of activities, such as party political broadcasts which are designed to gain your vote.

Polling station – a building designated for the day as a place where you can go to vote, for example, your local school.

MP – Member of Parliament. The elected party political candidate for your area.

Surgery – is, in this case, where you can go to consult your MP on problem issues in your area, for example, Housing.

Cabinet – Senior ministers in the government who are responsible for specific areas, such as health or education.

A polling station on election day

on a campaign for election. This will involve canvassing for votes, the production of election literature and, in national elections, party political broadcasts are used to promote and explain ideas.

Voting takes place on a stated day at a local polling station. Voting takes place by a secret ballot and the votes are taken in sealed boxes to a central counting place. After counting, the returning officer for the area then makes a public declaration of the results.

Parliament

Each MP is elected to serve an area of the country called a constituency for a maximum of five years. During that time, they debate issues at the Houses of Parliament at Westminster in London and are responsible for determining:

- taxes to fund public services
- laws, rules and regulations, relating to areas such as:
  - education
  - health
  - defence issues
  - law and order
  - international relations, and
  - home affairs.

MPs also hold regular surgeries in their constituencies.

What happens next?

After an election, the party which has gained the largest number of seats becomes the ruling party for the council or government for the next five years.

At local level: The council leader arranges for council members to vote for members of their executive.

At national level: The Prime Minister appoints a group of MPs to be ministers and help run the country. A group of senior ministers and secretaries of state form the Cabinet. The rest of the MPs who do not hold government office are known as backbenchers.

The political party that gained the second largest number of seats at the election becomes the official Opposition. The Leader of the Opposition will appoint members of their political party to act as Opposition spokespeople on specific aspects of government. This group of people become the Shadow Cabinet. All MPs who do not belong to the political party in power are opposition MPs.

Activities

1. Find out the following about your school's local MP:
   - name
   - party the MP represents
   - main beliefs
   - role in government.
2. Who is the Leader of the Opposition?

Conservative, Michael Portillo, losing his constituency (1997)

How national government works

Activity

Which of the parties would you support from the brief outline of their policies given below? Why?

The main political parties in Parliament

	The Labour Party	The Conservative Party	The Liberal Democrat Party
	 (founded in early 20th century)	 (founded in the 18th century)	 (founded in 1988)
Education	• believes in a close relationship between the public and private sectors, is committed to investment in education	• believes in a greater role for the private sector – private money should be added to public expenditure	• wants to increase income tax by 1p in the pound to invest in education
Health	• committed to investment and reducing waiting lists	• believes in a free market between health providers and hospitals as a way to improve performance	• wants to cut waiting lists; believes in free dental and eye tests
Europe	• committed to the single currency when the time is right for Britain	• is against the single currency though some of the party are pro-European and there has been friction	• believes that Britain should join the single currency as soon as possible
Electoral reform	• supports reform in line with the Jenkins Commission report (see page 51)	• believes firmly in the current system of first past the post	• is in favour of full electoral reform and the single transferable vote system

Figure 4.1 The main political parties in Parliament and their policies

The House of Commons

MPs sit in the House of Commons, the lower chamber of the British Parliament. The upper chamber is called the House of Lords. The main function of the House of Commons is to make the laws by which the country is governed and managed.

Debating in the House of Commons

An issue is debated by calling a motion in Parliament. At the end of each debate the Speaker (the MPs' chairperson) will ask those MPs in favour to say 'aye' and those against the motion to say 'no'. If there is no clear decision either way the Speaker will call a division. The division bell will sound in Parliament to alert those MPs who were not in the chamber that a division has been called. At least 40 MPs must vote before a decision can be made. Two MPs from each side of the debate act as tellers and count the votes. During a division the MPs go to the division lobbies, the 'ayes' to one side and the 'nos' to the other. At the end of the vote the Speaker will announce the result.

In Parliament the political parties ensure that MPs turn up to vote according to party policy by appointing officers called whips. The head of each party's whips is known as the Chief Whip.

Committees

A large amount of the work undertaken in Parliament is done by select committees which meet on a regular basis. Other committees are formed from time to time to deal with specific issues. These are called standing committees and they usually meet for a limited time. Committees make reports to the area of government service they meet to discuss or investigate.

The Cabinet

The Cabinet is a group of senior ministers who meet to determine the government's policy on issues and events. It also decides how issues will be dealt with and who will take the lead on important events.

A cabinet meeting

Leading members of the Cabinet include:

- the Deputy Prime Minister
- the Chancellor of the Exchequer who is responsible for the country's finance
- the Home Secretary, who is in charge of home affairs including the police force and keeping law and order
- the Foreign Secretary, who is responsible for international diplomacy and our relations with foreign countries
- the Secretary of State for Education, who is responsible for the state education system, its teachers and their performance
- senior ministers with responsibility for health, transport, defence, the environment, etc.

Activities

1 Many people think that the House of Commons is old-fashioned and needs updating. What do you think? Discuss this in groups.

2 Find out the names of the main members of the Cabinet.

The House of Lords

The upper chamber of the Houses of Parliament is the House of Lords which has existed as an institution of government since the 1300s. It consists of the Lords Spiritual (archbishops and bishops) and the Lords Temporal (life peers representing political parties, independent peers and hereditary peers). Reforms of the House of Lords are being prepared for consideration by Parliament.

The House of Lords has many functions. It debates issues of national importance which are not debated by the House of Commons. It considers bills which have been passed through the reading stages of the House of Commons and proposes amendments to the bills where appropriate. It is the final court of appeal in the British judicial system. The 26 law lords of the House of Lords have the final judgement on any case that they are required to consider. The law lords have the power to overturn a decision of the High Court and as such are the highest power in the British system.

The State Opening of Parliamant

The European Union

The European Union (EU) is made up of fifteen countries known as the member states. To be a member of the EU, countries must meet set criteria:

- their system of government must be democratic
- they must respect human rights
- they must operate a market economy which matches the economies of existing EU member states.

The EU is run by five main institutions along with the European Council. The European Council is a summit meeting, usually held twice a year, of the heads of government from each member state. Occasionally, the finance ministers or the foreign secretaries of the member states meet to discuss important issues. The European Council determines policy.

The five institutions of the EU are:

- The Council of Ministers
- The European Commission
- The European Parliament
- The European Court of Justice
- The European Court of Auditors.

The idea of the European Economic Community (EEC), created in 1957 by six countries, was to create a common market where labour, goods and services could be freely traded. The United Kingdom joined the EEC in 1973 and the EEC became the EU when the single market came into being in 1993. Since the UK became a member of the EU there has been a strong debate about whether it should continue its membership. Disagreements about the UK joining the single currency continue.

The Council of Ministers

This is the main decision-making body of the EU. It is made up of one representative of each member state who is usually an experienced and senior politician. The UK is represented by the foreign secretary. When important issues of a specific nature are being discussed, other ministers may replace the foreign secretary. Decisions are made by a straight majority vote. Any country has the right to veto a proposal that is against the national interests of the country.

Activities

1. Find the names of the fifteen member states of the EU.
2. Which organization of the EU holds the real power? Discuss.
3. The turnout of voters in the UK for European elections is low. Discuss the reasons for this.
4. Do you think that it is fair to set criteria for entry to the EU, or should anyone be able to join?

The European Commission

The European Commission is based in Brussels. Its main functions are:

- proposing policies and drafting laws
- ensuring that member states uphold EU treaties and implement policies
- managing the administration of the EU.

The EU has 20 commissioners and over 10 000 staff. Each country can appoint one commissioner. France, Spain, Germany, Italy and the UK have two commissioners. Although they are appointed by their countries, commissioners are expected to act independently of their elective governments. Commissioners specialize in different areas of EU policy.

The EU Parliament building

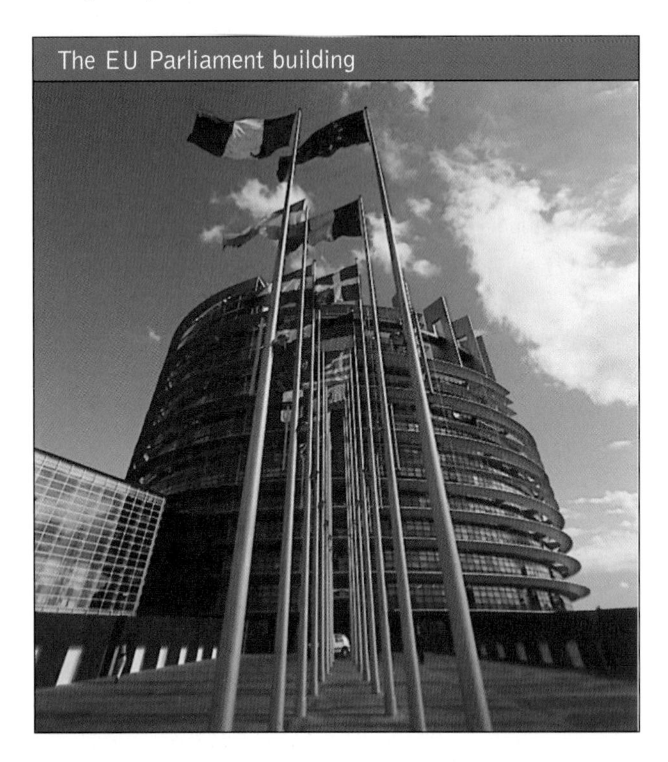

The European Parliament

The European Parliament meets in Strasbourg and Brussels. Representatives are called Members of the European Parliament (MEPs) and are elected to serve for a maximum of five years. Elections for the 626 MEPs are held in June. Since 1999 MEPs have been elected using proportional representation. MEPs represent a constituency which is larger than the area covered by a national government constituency.

The main function of the European Parliament is to consider the proposals put forward by the European Commission. Proposals are discussed by committees then reports are forwarded to the Parliament for debate and decision-making. The European Parliament is responsible for the standardization of European law and trade regulation across Europe. It is funded through negotiated contributions from national governments.

The European Court of Justice

The European Court of Justice is located in Luxembourg. It has fifteen judges, one from each member country. The court sits to consider disputes about EU laws. Its function is to resolve disputes, and to clarify the scope of EU laws. The European Court of Justice has the power to rule against a decision of a national government.

The European Court of Auditors

This organization monitors the financial management of the EU. Its main function is to look after the interests of the EU's taxpayers by ensuring that the EU's finance is being used for the purposes for which it was raised. It also helps the EU Parliament to check its annual budget spending. The Court of Auditors is made up of fifteen members, one from each country.

Activities

1. Find out the names of the two British European Commissioners.
2. Who is the MEP representing your area? Which MEP constituency do you live in?
3. Some people think the EU is bureaucratic and inefficient. Would you change any of the organizations within the EU? Why? Discuss.

Taking part in the democratic process

Elections

Everyone over the age of eighteen is invited annually to place their name on the register of electors which is compiled by the local council. This register tells the returning officer who controls the elections called in the area who is eligible to vote in an election. Members of the House of Lords and convicted prisoners are not allowed to vote. When an election is called the returning officer will contact each voter and invite them to vote at a prescribed polling station between set hours on the day of the election. The polling station will be managed by polling clerks who will ensure that a secret ballot is maintained and that each voter receives a specially stamped ballot paper on which to vote. The ballot paper names all of the candidates who are standing for election and the political parties which they represent, if appropriate.

Taking part – voting

The right to vote was introduced for all men in 1884. Women were not allowed to vote so the women's suffrage movement came into being. Women known as Suffragettes campaigned for a woman's right to vote. Many of them died in the cause of women's suffrage. Women over the age of 30 were given the vote in 1918. All women over the age of 21 were granted the right to vote in 1928.

Candidates standing for election must be 21 years of age and British citizens. Those who are members of the Anglican or Roman Catholic clergy, members of the House of Lords, civil servants, judges, and members of the armed services and the police cannot stand for election. Candidates have to be nominated by ten people who live in the constituency. Nomination forms must be returned to the returning officer by a set day. Candidates are required to pay the returning officer a deposit of £500, which is lost if a candidate fails to secure 5 per cent of the vote at the election. The returning officer then publishes the official candidates for the election. Most candidates represent political parties and have been the subject of a selection procedure. Some people stand as independent candidates but very few are elected to Parliament.

One of the benefits of a democracy is that the people are involved in choosing the people who will govern, and to some extent the content of the programme the government will undertake, by selecting their candidate from a political party whose manifesto meets the needs and aspirations of the voter. The voter turnout at local, parliamentary and European elections is falling. Many people argue that this is because the people don't have confidence in the present system. Some people think it is because people feel that all politicians are the same. Some people think that it is because voting is difficult under the current arrangement. Other people think that voting should be moved from its traditional spot on a weekday to a day at the weekend.

Figure 4.2

If you are unable to vote in person, you can apply for a postal vote or a proxy vote. If you vote by proxy you give another person the legal right to vote on your behalf. Voting by post requires you to complete a form and send it to the returning officer. In some areas where voter turnout is low, local councils have offered postal votes to voters.

Activities

1 Find the general election results for 1997 and 2001 for your constituency and compare the results.

2 What do you think are the reasons for the changes?

3 Find the results for the most recent local elections in your ward of the local council. Compare the results for the candidates of the different parties.

Every democracy tries to get its people involved by giving them information so they can make appropriate decisions and by giving them control over their own lives. A healthy democracy involves a majority of the people in discussion and decision making. Politicians from all political parties accept that there is a need for all people to be involved in the political system and that all parties should be proactive in increasing the number of people exercising their right to vote. At present, and historically, the predominant MP is male and white. Parliament is not representative of the ethnic or gender balance in the country. There has been some improvement in recent years but much remains to be done.

In recent years fewer young people have voted at general elections. The major political parties have enlisted the support of prominent personalities and pop stars to encourage young people to vote.

Referenda

Sometimes there is an issue of national importance that will affect people's lives. In instances like this a referendum may be held. Britain held a referendum in 1975 to decide whether or not to continue as a member of the Common Market. Some countries, such as Switzerland, use referenda far more regularly than other countries as they want to know how the citizens of the country feel about important issues.

People who support the use of referenda as a political tool have argued that this system gives more power to the ordinary people by allowing them to make decisions about issues which affect their lives. People who oppose referenda have argued that the system is expensive, that it can stop Parliament from operating smoothly and that there is no point in electing representatives if we do not let them get on with the job for which they were elected.

1975 Referendum poster

Referenda are worded as questions. It is important that the question is asked in an unambiguous way or the outcome could be confused. A question worded in a certain way might influence the outcome of the referendum.

Using the Internet

Since the introduction of the Internet as a tool in the lives of many, some people think that this should be used to consult the public about issues which affect them. They think that this would make consultation quick and efficient. Opponents argue that it is useful as a research tool to secure a person's initial response to issues, but that its use discriminates against those with no Internet facilities.

Local council consultation

Local councils have started to consult residents about important issues like new housing or road developments or proposed changes to the education system. They consult through meetings and documents and ask for public comment. Local people are often kept informed about the workings of their local council through local council news magazines.

Activities

1. Find out what issues your local council has consulted on in the past year.
2. Do you think that your local council consults enough?
3. Do you think referenda are a good way of increasing participation in the decision-making process? Discuss this in groups.
4. Britain does not use referenda as often as it should. Discuss.
5. If you were holding a referendum about drinking at the age of sixteen, how would you word the question you asked on the ballot paper?

How national government manages the economy

The government has to raise money to finance public spending, which is the money spent on health, education, defence, police and prisons, housing and other public services. The government raises its money through a system of taxation:

Direct taxation – Some taxes are raised through the income people earn. The rate of taxation changes according to how much people earn. Generally, the more money people earn, the more tax they pay. Income tax is the largest source of government income.

Indirect taxation – Value added tax (VAT) is an indirect tax. This does not depend on what people earn but is set at a fixed rate and is charged on goods and services. The person who sells the product or service adds the tax to the price, then pays the VAT to the government.

Proportional tax – stays at the same percentage regardless of how much people earn, for example, National Insurance Contributions. These are used to fund social security payments such as the state pension. There will be major changes to this area of taxation in the future.

The budget

Each year the government makes an economic statement about the levels of taxation for the coming year and the allowances for children, family and older people. This is known as the budget. The Chancellor of the Exchequer makes the budget statement to the House of Commons, usually in March. An interim budget statement is often given in November. The budget statement outlines the proposed spending targets the government has set for the next year and what measures the government will use to show that its targets have been met.

The way the government chooses to raise and allocate its finance will determine how people live. If the government raises direct taxation and raises VAT on goods then people will have less money to spend and save. By far the greatest amount of money spent by the government is on social security. This includes unemployment benefits, income support and pensions.

The Chancellor Gordon Brown on budget day

Figure 4.3

If the government does not increase state benefits regularly then many unemployed, disabled and ill people will find it more difficult to meet bills and health requirements. However, people with children will benefit indirectly if the government chooses to spend more on education. Similarly, the quality of life for many people is affected by how safe they feel in the community so the amount spent on law and order is important. Balancing the books and keeping the country safe and happy while caring for the sick and the disabled are some of the issues facing government.

Inflation

One of the measures used by the government in setting targets is the level of inflation. This refers to the amount by which the price of goods has increased in the past year. If the price of food has increased by 3 per cent in the last year then the inflation for food will be 3 per cent. The government sets targets for inflation to keep inflation under control. If the level of inflation is not controlled, prices spiral upwards and everyday goods become expensive for ordinary people. If inflation is allowed to fall too low, the economy might slow and the country might fall into a depression. This could mean job losses and less money to spend. It is important that the spending targets are accurate.

Government spending policy at work

Government spending

There are fifteen main government departments which rely on public money to function. Each year the government decides how much money will be spent in each department. The government decided in 1998 to set out a three-year spending plan. Some spending is index-linked, which means that it cannot rise above the level of inflation. This afast rate. Typical government spending is shown in Figure 4.4.

Education	12%
Social security	32%
Health and related services	17%
Housing, environment, heritage	5%
Industry, agriculture, employment	4%
Defence	7%
Law and order	5%
Transport	3%
Debt interest	8%
Other expenditure	7%

Figure 4.4 Typical government expenditure

Controlling government spending

The House of Commons has a duty to ensure that the government does not raise money through taxation without good cause. The budget proposals are presented to the House of Commons as a Finance Bill. This bill goes through the same stages as any other bill and it takes about four months for it to pass through the stages to become a Finance Act, a new act allowing the government to raise the money it needs. In this way the proposals for raising finance are discussed fully and examined carefully. The House of Commons also has a part to play in giving its permission for the government to spend the money it has raised. Each year the government prepares its estimates of departmental spending and places them before the House of Commons for approval. The House must approve the estimates before any department receives money. To check that the money given to departments of the government is spent correctly, a select committee, known as the Public Accounts Committee, meets and examines the accounts of each department to check that the money is being spent on the programmes for which it was raised.

Activities

1 If you were in charge of the exchequer what would your spending priorities be? Choose three and explain why you think they are important? What does the whole group think is important?

2 Which method of taxation do you think is fairer – direct taxes or indirect taxes?

Becoming a European citizen

The single currency

Britain joined the EEC in 1973. All three major political parties now broadly agree with the single market and Britain's membership of the EU but there is disagreement about Britain joining the single currency. On 1 January 2002, the euro became the unit of currency in the majority of member states of the EU. On 1 July 2002 it became the sole currency when old national currencies such as the German mark and the French franc were no longer legal tender. All EU countries qualify for membership of the single currency, though Britain and Denmark have chosen to opt out. Thirteen countries now use the euro. The euro is accepted as currency in some UK shops, for example Marks and Spencer.

Supporters of Britain joining the single currency have stated that the euro will establish greater stability in Europe. The removal of exchange rates will help businesses to plan, and as there would be no currency changes, costs would be lowered. This could lead to the creation of more jobs. Opponents of the single currency state that it does not allow for the differences in growth rate between countries as the euro has the same value throughout the EU. They also think it removes national sovereignty because decisions relating to European finance will be made centrally rather than by individual member states.

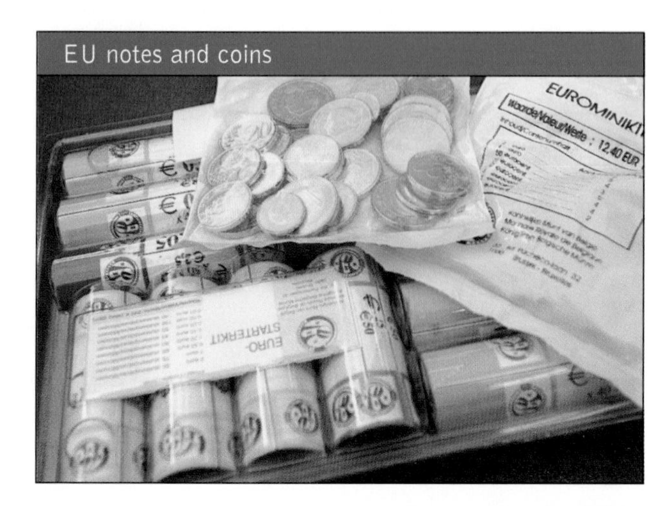

EU notes and coins

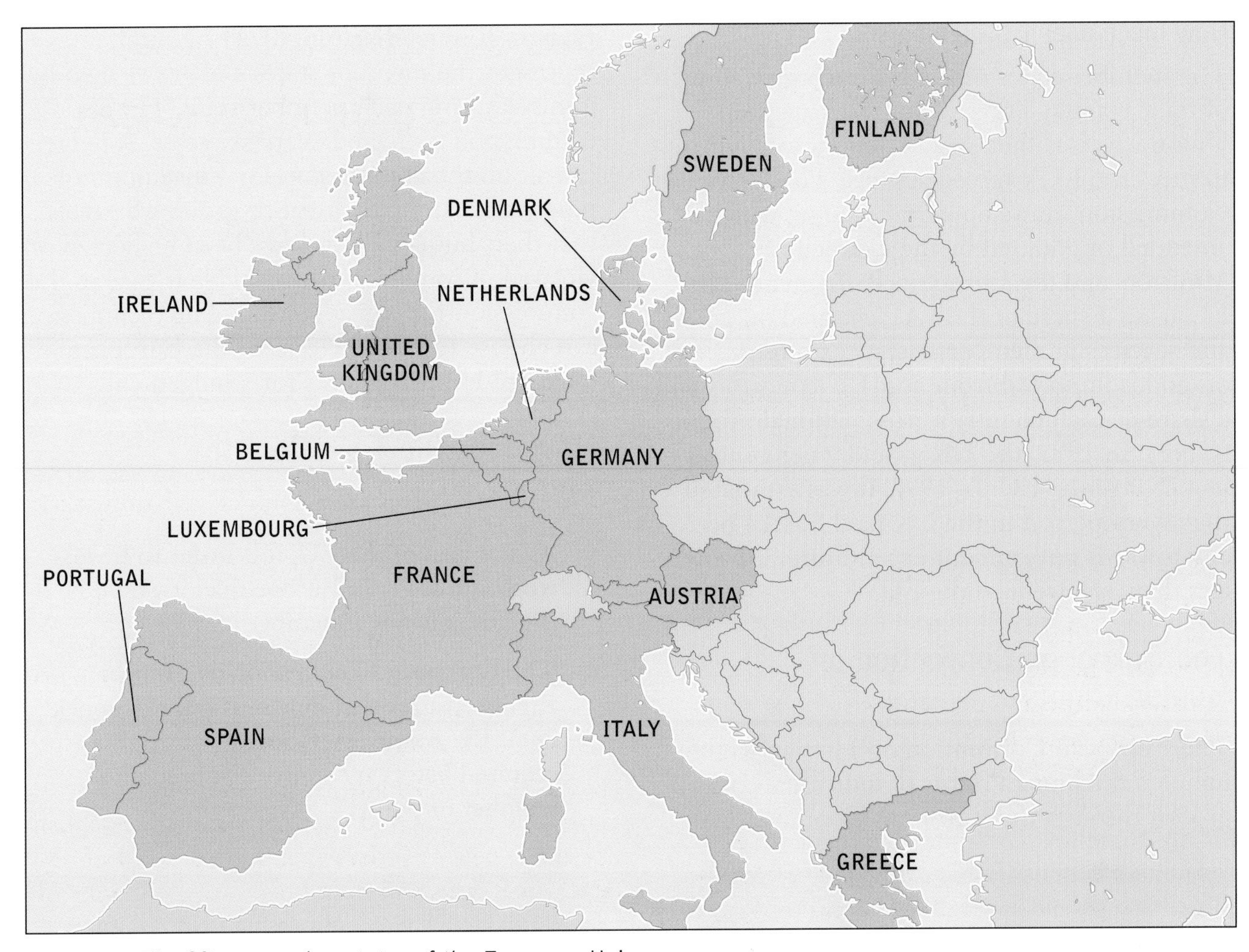

Figure 4.4 The fifteen member states of the European Union

The EU budget

The budget for the EU is set each year by the European Parliament and the Council of Ministers. An example of EU income is shown in Figure 4.5.

Customs duties	15%
VAT	42%
National contributions	40%
Levies on agricultural products	3%

Figure 4.5 EU income

Some countries such as Greece, Ireland and Portugal receive more from the EU than they contribute. The UK and Germany put more money in than they take out. They are known as 'net contributors' to the EU budget.

An example of EU expenditure is shown in Figure 4.6.

Structural measures (fisheries, farms, regional, social, infrastructure)	35.5%
Agriculture	46%
Administration	5%
Overseas aid	6.5%
Research and technology	4%
Miscellaneous	3%

Figure 4.6 EU expenditure

How much does EU membership cost?

The member states of the EU each give some of their country's revenue to the European Union which is then re-distributed to countries to meet the EU's agreed actions. The European Commission draws up a draft budget which is amended or adopted by the Council of Ministers and the European Parliament. The EU takes a share of the VAT charged on goods and services in member states, customs duties on goods imported from non-EU countries and a share of each country's gross national product (GNP). In 1993, the UK gave 0.9 per cent of its GNP to the EU. In 1997, it was estimated that every person in the UK paid £12.14 per day towards government expenditure. Of this, less than 37p went to the EU.

The European Convention on Human Rights

The European Convention on Human Rights upholds the human rights of individuals or groups through the European Commission of Human Rights. The judges, 41 in number, represent the member states and are elected by ministers from each member state. The commission is elected every six years. A judge can sit on the commission for a maximum of nine years. Any individual or group who feels that their human rights have been neglected or violated in some way can refer their case to the commission for consideration. The commission can choose to pass the case to the European Court of Human Rights for a judgement.

How does the EU affect the average citizen?

- As a citizen of the EU, it is easier to travel, work and study in Europe than it would be if the UK was not a member of the EU.
- The European Commission on Human Rights ensures that human rights are upheld in all EU countries. Good human rights are required before a country can become a member of the EU.

The Eurostar makes it easier to travel to Europe

European standards at work

- The EU has a set of rules which apply to consumer goods across the EU.
- Food labelling and safety regulations for toys and electrical goods must be adhered to by all member states.
- The EU gives funds for projects in poorer regions to develop economies so all member states can benefit.
- The EU has developed programmes to improve the environment. These projects include reducing air pollution, promoting public transport, establishing basic water and bathing standards, reducing noise emissions in the community and the workplace, disposing of nuclear materials and chemicals safely, and the creation of environmentally sensitive areas to protect forests and natural habitats.

Activities

1. Do you think that the UK should stay a part of the EU? Give reasons for your answer.
2. Do you think the UK should join the single currency? Why?
3. With a partner discuss the benefits of EU membership.
4. What do you consider to be the three main advantages to the UK of EU membership?

Young Germans, protesting against transportation of nuclear waste

Trade and the EU

In 1994, the European Economic Area (EEA) was created from the members of the EU and other countries in Europe. It was established to strengthen the free trade links between European countries and the rest of the world. In 1994, the EU did 59 per cent of its trade with other EU countries. The UK did 52 per cent of its trade with its European partners. In international agreements it is important that the EU acts as a single powerful unit rather than individual countries negotiating on their own especially with big trading partners such as Japan and the USA.

Check it out

What you should have learned from this chapter

Look at the areas of study in the table. You should now know and understand the terminology and concepts that we have explored in Chapter 4: National and European government.

The activities and questions in the chapter, and the extra sheets your teacher will have worked through with you, should have helped you to learn about this topic.

If some of the areas are not clear, read through the pages again. If you are still not sure, ask your teacher to explain them again.

Area of study	Page
Understanding how the UK is governed	62
How national government works	64
The institutions of the European Union	67
Voting and political parties	69
The budget and taxation	72
Government spending	73
Becoming a European citizen	74
Trade and the EU	77

You should be able to answer all the following questions. These are short answer questions similar to those that will appear in Section A of the written exam paper that you will sit at the end of the course.

The knowledge and concepts covered in this chapter will also be tested in longer, more detailed questions in Sections B and D of the exam paper.

?

1. Name the five institutions of the EU.
2. Where does the European Parliament meet?
3. List the functions of the European Commission.
4. Define a democracy.
5. Explain the difference between a referendum and an election.
6. What is a register of electors?
7. What system is used in the UK to elect MPs and MEPs?
8. Name three political parties in the UK.
9. What are taxes?
10. What is the European Economic Area (EEA)?
11. Which committee monitors government spending?

5 Criminal and civil law

How does the law affect you?

As a child your rights under the law are restricted, but as you get older the law requires you to do more things for yourself and to accept responsibility for your own actions. Figure 5.1 indicates what you can do at certain ages.

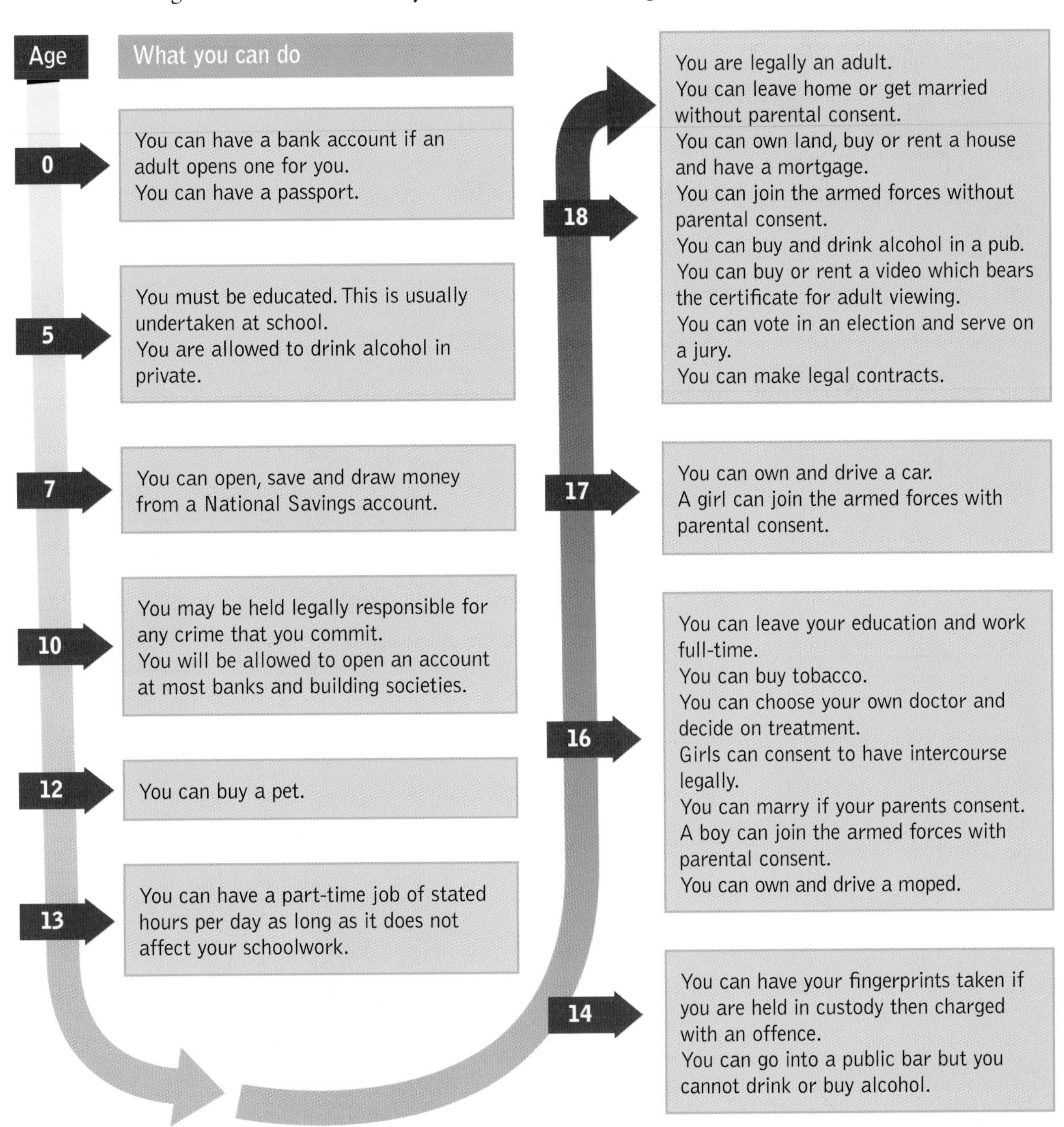

Figure 5.1 What the law allows you to do, from age 0–18

Delivering papers earns this 13 year old money and leaves time for school

Activity

Discuss why you think a person's rights are determined by their age in the eyes of the law. For example, why must you be 12 years old to buy a pet?

Parents' duties

Your parents have a duty and a responsibility to look after you. They should make sure that you are properly fed and clothed. If you are ill, then they must ensure that you receive medical treatment. Your parents must send you to school or ensure that you receive a proper education. This is known as parental responsibility and though these responsibilities are not set out in law, society expects parents to give appropriate care and protection to children. Parental responsibility ends when a child becomes an adult at the age of eighteen. From this time parents advise their children.

Facts about life at home

- Your parents have a duty to discipline you and can decide how to punish you. Any physical punishment should not be too harsh.
- Your parents have the right to determine how you will be educated and which school you will attend.
- Your parents will determine which doctor and dentist you will see and which treatment you need.
- If your parents split up a court will decide who you will live with. The court will take your views into account.
- If your parents split up you have the right to have contact with both parents unless a court rules against this.
- Your parents have the right to determine which religion you will follow until you are old enough to decide this for yourself.
- If you live with foster parents they have a duty to look after you but they do not have the rights of your natural parents. A child who has been fostered for five years cannot return to their natural parents without the permission of a court.
- If you are adopted you get new parents who have the legal status of natural parents. At the age of eighteen you have the right to see a copy of your original birth certificate.

This little girl's first day at school

A check-up at the doctors

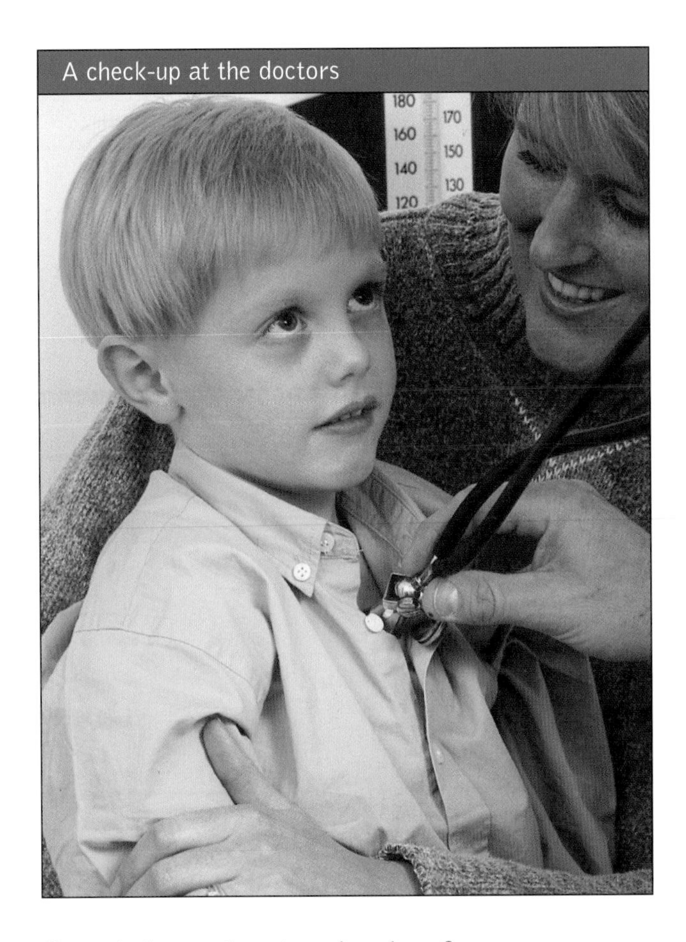

Activities

Discuss the following four statements:

- Children should be allowed to choose their own medical treatment from the age of twelve.
- Children should choose their secondary school.
- Smacking is a good way to discipline children.
- All children should receive £5 pocket money at eleven years of age.

Say why you agree or disagree with them.

Breakdown in standards of care

If parents do not care for their children appropriately or if they neglect or are cruel to them, then they may be taken to court. The court will decide what to do. It may decide to take the children from their parents and give the power to determine their care to someone else. Care is usually given to the local authority, but it could be invested in a family member. The parents may be allowed to keep control of the children's care with restrictions and checks on their behaviour. If a child is taken into local authority care their needs will be assessed by the local authority and they may live in a children's home or with foster parents. When a child is in local authority care the local authority and the parents share responsibility for the child's emotional and physical needs. The law tries to take the wishes of the child into account and social workers, doctors, solicitors and carers will try to put the interests of the child first.

Consumers and the law

A consumer is someone who buys goods and services. A consumer makes an agreement or deal with the person selling the goods. This agreement is a contract in law. Your rights as a consumer are laid down in laws such as the Trades Descriptions Act 1968, the Sale of Goods Act 1979 and the Supply of Goods and Services Act 1982. Advice and information about consumer affairs can be sought from the Office of Fair Trading. Specific problems can be referred to a Local Authority Trading Standards Department or Environmental Health Department.

The EU and the consumer

With the free movement of goods, consumers have a far wider choice. There are common rules to be followed by all European producers to ensure that all products placed on the UK market are safe and respect the minimum hygiene and quality standards. Contrary to what we read in the press and hear on the news, the EU is not in the business of telling the UK what it should produce and how it should do it. The directives from Brussels about the correct shape of bananas, strawberries and cucumbers are aimed at ensuring that fruit and vegetables are classified according to quality to facilitate trade and price comparisons. To ensure that standards of hygiene and safety are maintained, the EU has rulings on toys, packaging for household appliances, clear labelling procedures and hygiene requirements for food processing. In addition the EU brought in protection against unfair selling practices and travelling problems. One directive gives the consumer a 'cooling-off' period of one week when they can decide not to purchase any item if the sale was negotiated at home. The other directive ensures that, when travelling, the buyer is protected by compensation.

Street trading

The Supply of Goods and Services Act 1982 – the person providing a service must have the required skill to do so to an appropriate standard and must provide the service within a reasonable timescale. A pre-arranged price will be paid for the service.

The Supply of Goods and Services Act 1978 – goods must be of 'merchantable quality', fit for the purpose and described in full by the seller, by display or on the package. This law covers goods wherever they are bought – on the doorstep, from a street trader, by mail order or from a retail outlet. It applies to sale items and special offers though consumers should expect goods marked as 'seconds' to be inferior in quality. If goods are broken or faulty, the seller is responsible for the goods and should arrange for a refund or exchange.

The Trades Descriptions Act 1968 – it is an offence for a shopkeeper or trader to knowingly give a false description of the goods or services which they supply or of the use to which the goods can be put. Problems encountered should be referred to a Trading Standards Officer.

Activities

1. Write to the Trading Standards Officer at your local council to find out about how trading standards affect local businesses.
2. Watch the programme *Watchdog* and list some of the consumer stories which they investigate on behalf of the general public. Discuss the issues in each story and how they go against consumer law.

Young people and employment

The law for young people in employment changes at different ages. In all cases there is a requirement that any employment will not interfere with schoolwork so a young person should have the permission of the school before undertaking employment. Information about the number of hours young people can work at each age is available from the local careers office or an Educational Welfare Officer. Until the age of thirteen a young person can only be employed in entertainment, for example a pantomime with a special licence, or to do jobs at home for their parents, including agricultural work. Young people are eligible for full-time employment at the age of sixteen and can do part-time work from the age of thirteen. This work must not start before 7 am or finish later than 7 pm. They can work for up to two hours on a school day or a Sunday and longer on a Saturday. No employer can ask them to undertake any job which involves heavy lifting or moving which could cause injury.

Working for a living

Activities

1. Obtain a copy of the regulations relating to the employment of young people from your local careers office. Do you think that these restrictions require updating?
2. How many of the young people you know who work break these restrictions? Why do you think this happens?

The law and discrimination

The law gives everyone equal rights. Laws protect people from discrimination on the grounds of race, sex or disability. Proving discrimination can be difficult as it is necessary to prove that the actions of an individual, group of individuals or institution led to less favourable treatment and that discrimination was the result.

Types of discrimination

Direct discrimination occurs when a person is treated less favourably than their direct counterpart. This might refer to pay, career opportunities or number of hours worked.

Indirect discrimination occurs when the conditions required for a job cannot be applied equally to all people. For example, if a company only employs people who take a size 43 shoe or above, it may be discriminating against women.

Protecting people – The Social Chapter

The Social Chapter is a charter of fundamental rights for workers. It was felt that many groups of people in the workplace did not have the same rights as permanent full-time workers and that something needed to be done to restore

Racial discrimination

The Race Relations Act 1976 was implemented to prevent racial discrimination. It makes it illegal to discriminate on the grounds of ethnic origin or colour in matters relating to employment, education, housing, and the provision of goods and services. It is an offence under the Public Order Act to promote any activity that is 'likely to incite racial hatred'.

Sex discrimination

The Sex Discrimination Acts 1975 and 1986 state that it is unlawful to treat anyone on the grounds of their sex less favourably than a person of the opposite sex. Care should be taken when a job is advertised to choose wording which ensures that both males and females are encouraged to apply. The Act also states that services provided in the community should be of the same standard when offered to males and females. It is unlawful to offer inferior services to one group.

Disability discrimination

It is illegal to discriminate against someone with a disability in matters relating to employment, education, housing, public services and public transport. **The 1995 Disability Discrimination Act** strengthened the rights of people in employment. A firm cannot discriminate when recruiting, training, promoting and dismissing. In addition, employers must make adjustments to the workplace that would enable a person with a disability to do the job. Discrimination would result if their failure to comply with the Act could be proved. This applies to firms with 20 or more employees.

the balance. The aim was to improve the living and working conditions of EU citizens. These rights included:

- employment rights for part-time and temporary workers
- the right to annual paid holiday and the right to daily and weekly minimum rest periods for day-time and night work
- the right for men and women to have equal treatment – equal pay for equal work
- protection for pregnant women and nursing mothers, the right to a minimum period of leave, time off for examinations and job protection while pregnant
- the right to health and safety protection including protective clothing and first-aid facilities
- improved social and professional integration for disabled people. This includes enhanced opportunities for employment and to facilitate disabled access to the workplace.

Equal opportunity at work

Activity

Write to your local Citizens Advice Bureau or Law Centre and ask for information about discrimination that would be useful for people who feel they have been discriminated against.

What is crime?

If something is unlawful or illegal then it is an offence against the law of the land. This means that it is a crime. It is generally accepted that there are two main types of crime: crime which involves people and crime which involves property. Crimes against people include assault and murder. Crimes against property include vandalism and arson.

Attitudes to crime have changed over the years. In the nineteenth century it was possible to be imprisoned for stealing bread. Today a fine would probably be imposed. People in different countries hold differing views about what constitutes a crime. What is a crime in Britain may not be a crime somewhere else. For example, in Holland, smoking cannabis in public is acceptable, but this is not allowed in Britain. Even within Britain people's attitudes to crime vary. What one group finds acceptable others may consider criminal.

Some people believe that the increase in crime is connected to the growth of materialism (wanting to possess more things). Others think that it is connected to factors such as the breakdown in the nuclear and extended family, the decline of religious observance and the corresponding decline in moral standards, unemployment, activities on film and television which put crime and criminals on a pedestal, or drinking and drug-taking. The reasons why people commit crimes are complex and the majority of offenders are male, although female crime is on the increase.

Guarding against crime

The police force is the public's front-line defence against crime and criminals. The main duties of the police force are:

- to prevent and detect crime
- to protect life and property
- to maintain public order.

The police force needs the co-operation and support of the public to undertake its duties efficiently. A major part of these duties is to ask questions and to search property. The Police and Criminal Evidence Act 1984 sets out the police duties and powers.

A police officer, working with the community

The police have the power to stop people and search them in certain situations. If you are stopped by a police officer you can ask their name and the police station from which he or she works. You can ask why you have been stopped. You should give your name and address if the officer informs you that he or she considers that you have committed an arrestable offence. You do not have to answer any questions at this stage.

The police can search you after you have been arrested or if you are suspected of carrying:

- anything that could be used for a burglary or theft
- stolen goods
- drugs
- weapons, or anything that could be used as a weapon.

The officer should explain why you are being searched and what he or she expects to find.

Activities

1. Some people believe that the power to stop and search is abused. Other people think that the police should be able to stop and search at random. Discuss this.
2. What would Britain be like without a police force? Think about the main duties of the police and what would happen if there was no police force to carry them out.
3. The police are our protectors. Do you agree with this statement?
4. Should everyone be able to see police information? Think about what effect this might have on a person's employment and family life.

Helping the police

Everyone should be prepared to help the police to keep law and order and to ensure the safety of the public. However, if the police ask you to help them with their enquiries, you should ask if you are being arrested. If you are asked to help voluntarily, you have the right to refuse, but if the police arrest you, you must go with them. When you arrive at the police station, you have the right to send a message to a friend or a family member to let them know where you are. You have the right to advice from a solicitor. The police cannot question a person under the age of sixteen without a parent or an appropriate adult being present. You must give your name and address, but you do not have to answer any questions. Helping the police with their enquiries does not always mean that the person being questioned is accused of the offence.

A police officer at the station's front desk

Being arrested

If you have been arrested and charged with an offence, you may be:

- reprimanded, or given a warning or caution. A police officer talks to you about the offence and explains what will happen if you break the law again. The police will keep a record of the crime. Only people who have admitted they have broken the law can be reprimanded or cautioned. If you have committed three offences, you will automatically face prosecution for the third offence.
- prosecuted. Your case will be referred to court for consideration. If you are found guilty and sentenced, you will have a criminal record.

Police records

The police collect a wide range of information on people. The information is stored on the Police National Computer. The computer data is available at every police station. The information includes people who have been arrested, people who have reported crimes, criminals, witnesses, etc. If you have committed a crime between the ages of ten and seventeen, the police will hold your record until you are seventeen. If you are over seventeen, the record stays active for five years if you are reprimanded or charged with a recordable offence.

Checking up on the police

The Police and Criminal Evidence Act has guidelines to ensure that the police act within the law. Officers will be disciplined if they:

- neglect their duty
- make a false statement
- misuse their authority
- are abusive to a member of the public
- display racial discrimination.

Anyone who wishes to complain about the police can get information from the Police Complaints Authority.

Law-making in action

As we have already learned, one of the main functions of the House of Commons is to make the laws of the land. Laws are made so that it is easier for society to work as everyone is governed by the same set of rules. Before a law is made, it must go through a long process in Parliament. A proposal to change a law or to make a new law is put before Parliament as a bill. Bills can be proposed by individual MPs but they are usually presented to Parliament by the government. A bill proposed by an individual MP is known as a private member's bill. A bill goes through a set procedure before it becomes an Act of Parliament.

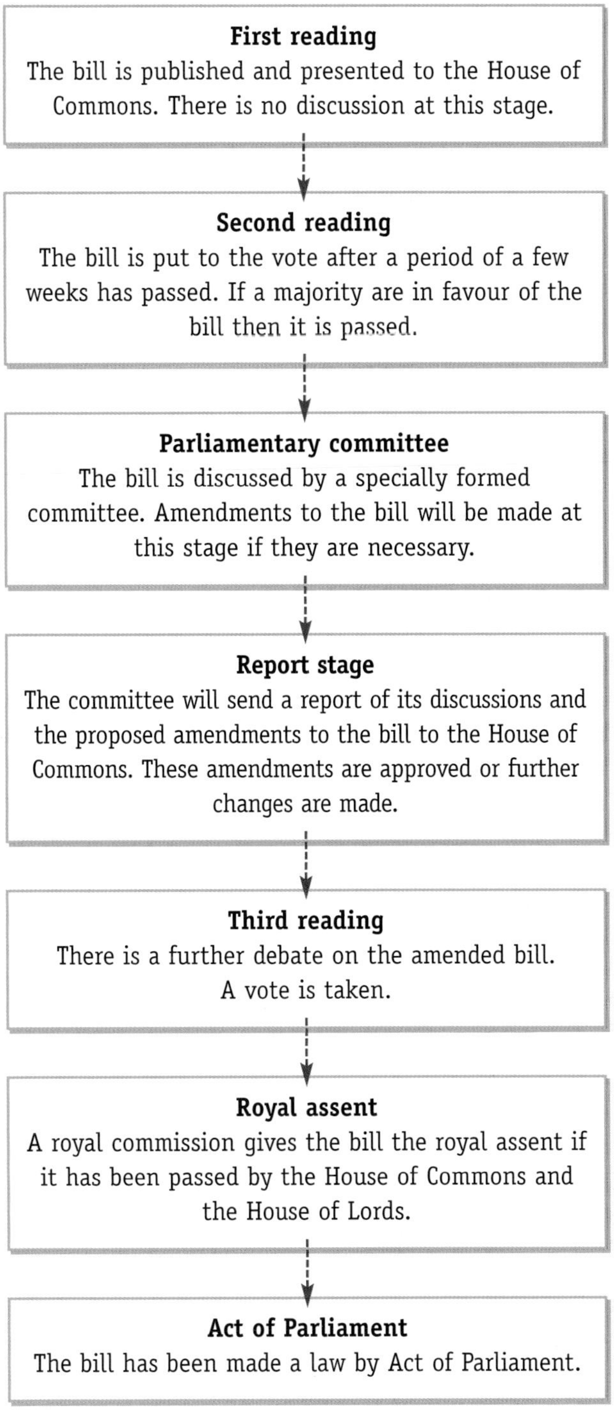

First reading
The bill is published and presented to the House of Commons. There is no discussion at this stage.

↓

Second reading
The bill is put to the vote after a period of a few weeks has passed. If a majority are in favour of the bill then it is passed.

↓

Parliamentary committee
The bill is discussed by a specially formed committee. Amendments to the bill will be made at this stage if they are necessary.

↓

Report stage
The committee will send a report of its discussions and the proposed amendments to the bill to the House of Commons. These amendments are approved or further changes are made.

↓

Third reading
There is a further debate on the amended bill. A vote is taken.

↓

Royal assent
A royal commission gives the bill the royal assent if it has been passed by the House of Commons and the House of Lords.

↓

Act of Parliament
The bill has been made a law by Act of Parliament.

Figure 5.2 How laws are made

To become an Act of Parliament a bill must pass through all stages of the procedure in both the House of Commons and the House of Lords. Most bills are passed with agreement between the Houses of Parliament. Where there is a disagreement, the House of Lords can delay a bill for a period of up to a year. The House of Lords cannot delay a financial bill.

Activities

1 Do you think that the process for making a new law is satisfactory? What changes, if any, would you make?

2 Do you think that we should change our method of government to make it easier to change laws? What system would you have?

Types of law in Britain

Laws in Britain have been made over the years in a variety of ways.

- Statutes are laws that have been made by Parliament.
- Common law includes laws that have been passed down through the ages. Everyone knew these laws and the courts based their decisions upon them.
- Bylaws are made by local councils and some public agencies. They govern local matters such as litter, dog fouling or other anti-social behaviour.

When laws are passed, it is up to the legal system to determine how they should operate in practice. If a case is presented to court for a decision, the judge will investigate other cases to see if there has been a similar case in the past. The judge's decision will be based on the interpretation of the law in the previous case. This is known as case law. Where there is no previous case to take into consideration, the judge will make the interpretation of the law. The judge will create the precedent against which future cases will be considered.

Judges, on their way to court

European laws

The European government also makes laws. The European Commission prepares a proposal for the proposed new law and sends it to the European Parliament where it is discussed. The European Parliament may amend the proposal. After discussion and amendment the proposal is returned to the European Commission so that it can be drafted into a firm proposal and sent to the European Council for consideration. The Council discusses the proposal and can choose to make amendments. The council members will consult with their national governments for approval to move to a 'common position' on the proposal with other member states. Once a 'common position' is reached, the proposal will be discussed by the European Parliament. Once the European Parliament has approved the proposal the Council adopts it as European Law. If the European Parliament rejects the proposal, it can still become law if all members of the European Council agree to it.

European laws apply to all member countries. They are known as regulations. Sometimes the European Union will issue a 'directive' to member countries. The directive will instruct member states to introduce the new law within a set time limit.

How does European law become UK law?

European law is translated into national law in Westminster. Proposals from the European Commission are sent to London and discussed by senior civil servants. At the same time the proposals will be discussed by the civil servants representing national government in Brussels. The proposals will be considered by the UK's minister for Europe and the relevant select committees in the House of Lords and the House of Commons. Finally the proposals are presented to Parliament for consideration.

I'll see you in court!

In Britain, there are two types of law:

- Civil law relates to people's private rights, for example boundary disputes and marital breakdown.
- Criminal law relates to crimes which are against the law of the land and which have been made by government statute.

Each set of laws is heard in its own court system. Each court has its own procedure and practice.

Figure 5.3

Civil law

Because civil law relates to disputes concerning contracts or agreements with another person over a private matter, the matter is often dealt with by a solicitor without going to court. These cases are said to have been settled 'out of court'. Even when the matter is referred to court, in certain circumstances your solicitor can represent you so your presence is not always necessary.

Dealing with civil cases

Civil cases are referred to county courts for consideration. In these cases one individual takes action against another. We call the person taking the action 'the plaintiff' and the person against whom the action is being taken 'the defendant'. In such cases the plaintiff is said to be 'suing' the defendant. The court will judge the defendant to be 'liable' or 'not liable'. When a defendant is found to be liable, the court will make a judgement and the defendant will be required to comply with the judgement or may appeal against the decision. The defendant is usually required to pay 'damages' to the plaintiff, which are a form of compensation. In county courts, the cases are heard by a judge who decides on the facts and the law.

A county court

County courts deal with contracts up to a certain sum, undefended divorces, small claims of less than £5000 and equitable issues, for example disputes about wills, settlements and trusts, bankruptcy. A higher level of civil court deals with larger issues. Contracts will be referred to the Queen's Bench division, property disputes and complex equitable issues are referred to the Chancery Division and complex divorces and disputes are heard by the Family Division. If a person feels that they were not dealt with fairly they may appeal against the decision. The issue would be referred to the Court of Appeal. The final appeal could be referred to the House of Lords if it was considered to be of public importance.

Criminal law

Criminal law relates to matters such as theft, assault, rape, drug offences, violence and murder. Because criminal law deals with offences against society, offenders are prosecuted by the Crown Prosecution Service whose aim is to protect individuals and society from crime. The aim of the prosecution is to punish the offender, if that person is found guilty. The law determines the punishment to be given.

Dealing with criminal cases

The majority of cases of criminal law are heard in magistrates' courts. However, all cases begin in magistrates' courts even if they are passed immediately to the crown court for the trial, verdict and sentence. In these instances the case is heard by the magistrates' court in what are known as 'committal proceedings'. Most towns have a magistrates' court so they usually deal with local cases.

Magistrates' courts are held by magistrates or 'justices of the peace' (JPs). JPs are appointed and work unpaid. Cases are heard by a bench of magistrates. If the person is found guilty the sentence will be decided from a set range of sentences for the crime committed. In court the magistrates are supported on matters of law by a clerk of court, as generally magistrates have no formal legal training.

Trial by jury

When a case is held at a crown court it is heard by a judge and jury. Usually the defendant has pleaded not guilty. If the defendant had pleaded guilty at the preliminary hearing, the judge would have passed sentence immediately.

During the trial, the prosecution puts its case, presents evidence and, where appropriate, calls witnesses. The defence then makes its case, presents evidence and calls witnesses. The prosecution and the defence barristers will cross-question each other's witnesses during the trial. The judge will then sum up the case for the jury and will take the opportunity to advise them on any relevant points of law. The jury will retire to consider the case in private. When a decision has been made the jury will return to court and the foreman will deliver the verdict. If the accused is found guilty, the judge will pronounce the sentence of the court. If the accused is found not guilty, the judge will discharge the case.

Statue of Justice on the Old Bailey dome, London

The rights of accused people

In the British legal system, a person accused of a crime has rights set down in law. These rights apply to every case.

- A person is assumed innocent until proven guilty.
- Except in youth court cases, the case will be heard in public.
- The court has a duty to listen to the accused and his/her lawyer as long as the content is relevant to the defence of the case.
- Witnesses must give evidence in the presence of the accused. The accused has the right to ask questions of the witnesses after they have completed their evidence.
- Proof of the crime the accused is alleged to have committed must be beyond all reasonable doubt.
- The prosecution must prove the charge against the accused.
- Once a person has been tried and a decision has been reached on whether to convict, the person cannot be charged with this particular offence again.

People in the legal system

Judges

Judges must be qualified barristers or solicitors and are nominated or appointed by the Lord Chancellor. Judges do not yet represent our society as they are mainly middle-class, white and male.

Solicitors and barristers

The legal profession in England and Wales is divided into two branches of professionals: solicitors and barristers. There are many more solicitors in practice than barristers. A barrister usually has no direct contact with the public; it is a solicitor who retains, instructs and pays the barrister. A barrister will also be briefed by the Crown Prosecution Service to act on its behalf in court.

Solicitors work with clients who may need legal advice relating to accident claims, matrimonial problems, tax, land laws, conveyancing, making a will, civil litigations, crime or commercial work. Solicitors may work in private practice or for local authorities, the civil service, industry and commerce, or large organizations such as trade unions, public bodies and charities.

A barrister is primarily a specialist in advocacy, that is to say the presentation of the client's case to the court or tribunal which has to decide it. Barristers need to have a detailed knowledge of the law, good judgement and the ability to present a case clearly. They will also prepare every case thoroughly.

Activities

1. Try to arrange to visit the public gallery of a court. Make notes about events.
2. Should judges hear criminal cases without a jury. What are the advantages and disadvantages? Discuss.

Jury

A jury is selected randomly from the current electoral register. A jury consists of twelve adults between the ages of 18 and 70. The following people cannot sit on a jury:

- those who have been to prison in the last ten years
- those who have been on probation in the last five years
- ministers of religion
- lawyers
- police officers.

Crown Prosecution Service

People who commit criminal acts are prosecuted by the crown, that is the state. Before 1986, prosecutions were brought by the police. Since then an independent agency called the Crown Prosecution Service (CPS) has decided which cases to prosecute. The CPS is led by the Director of Public Prosecutions.

Youth courts

Children under the age of ten cannot be charged with a criminal offence. Children under sixteen must be accompanied by a parent when their case is heard in court. If young people under the age of eighteen are charged with a criminal offence, the case will be heard in a youth court. If the young person is charged with a serious offence, the matter may be referred to a crown court for trial. Members of the public are not allowed into a youth court and the defendant must not be named in any press coverage. Magistrates who consider youth cases are specially trained to deal with the issues in a more informal manner.

Activities

1. Why do you think youth courts differ from magistrates' courts?
2. Are the accused people in youth courts protected at the expense of the victims? Discuss.

The European Court

Inside the European Court of Justice

The European Court of Justice was set up in 1952. By 1985 it was hearing 400 cases a year and it asked the European Council to consider setting up another judicial body to help with the work. The Court of First Instance was set up in 1989.

The Court of Justice comprises fifteen judges and eight advocates general. The Court of First Instance is composed of fifteen judges. Both sit in chambers of three to five judges.

Jurisdiction

It is the responsibility of the Court of Justice to ensure that the law (of the EU) is observed in the interpretation of the treaties establishing the European Union and of the provisions laid down by the various EU institutions. The Court of Justice rules on the law, that is to say it declares what the relevant EU law is. The national court to which that ruling is addressed must apply the law as interpreted by the Court of Justice, without modification. The court deals with:

- actions for failure to fulfil Treaty obligations
- actions for damages
- actions for failure to act on European Council rulings
- preliminary rulings on the interpretation or validity of European law
- appeals against judgements of the Court of First Instance.

The Court of First Instance has the power to rule at the first instance on:

- items of annulment (where a member state, the European Council or commission asks for part of existing legislation to be deleted)
- actions brought against the commission under the Treaty
- disputes between the EU and its officials and workers.

More information on the European Court and its procedures, and also on how the European Court affects the lives of its citizens can be found at:

www.heinemann.co.uk/hotlinks

Case study: Criminal law – robbery

All too often, we hear how elderly people are attacked in their homes or in the street for their savings or pensions. Often the victim is beaten. If the victim suffers from shock, it can have long-lasting and severe effects on their future health and confidence. The incident recorded below is typical of such an attack.

The charges

Robbery in the eyes of the law is stealing by using, or threatening to use, force. Mugging involves violence when stealing and is robbery in the eyes of the law. Bodily harm can be actual or grievous (more serious). Both are considered serious offences by the police.

Sentence for robbery

For a robbery the court could choose one of the following sentences for a person under the age of seventeen:

- community service – up to 120 hours if the offender is sixteen and up to 240 hours if the offender is seventeen or above. Offenders must be sixteen to do community service.
- probation – offenders must be seventeen to do probation, which can be set from six months to three years.
- a combination of probation and community service.

Robbery of an elderly man

Harry is an 84-year-old retired welder who lives in a bungalow in a warden controlled complex on the outskirts of a small town. Harry is a widower. His two daughters live in the town with their families. All of the people in this small cul-de-sac are elderly and they rely on each other and their warden in times of distress for support.

One cold night in December, Harry had a heavy cold and was finding it difficult to sleep. He was watching News 24 on television at about 3.30 am when there was a knock on the door. When he answered the door, he found a young man with blood around his face. Harry helped the young man into his house and sat him in front of the fire. Before he could get the young man a drink of water, he was attacked from behind by two youths. Everything happened so quickly, he did not see enough of his attackers to give a clear description. Harry cried out for help as the intruders punched and kicked him.

Jenny lives across the road from Harry. She pulled the emergency cord to summon help from the warden. Mary, the warden, and her husband, Jeff, responded to Jenny's emergency call. When they arrived at Jenny's house, they saw three youths running away from Harry's home. As the complex is well lit they were able to see the three youths clearly. Jeff went into Harry's home and found him unconscious on the floor. Jeff called the police and ambulance to attend the scene. Harry's pension, which he had collected that day, was missing. Harry was taken to hospital where he was kept for four days for observation. His wounds needed eight stitches.

After a thorough police investigation, Mary and Jeff were able to identify the three young people. The young men aged fourteen, fifteen and sixteen were charged with robbery and occasioning grievous bodily harm. They pleaded not guilty to the charges and their case was referred to a youth court for consideration.

- curfew order – the offender is required to be indoors by a certain time at night for a set period.
- binding order – the offender promises never to offend again. If they do, they are punished for the old offence and the new one.
- supervision order – the offender has to be supervised or looked after and helped by a social worker or someone from a youth offending team for up to three years.
- attendance centre order – the offender has to attend a set centre for a number of hours at particular times. Attendance can be set from 12 to 36 hours.
- fine – the amount will depend on the seriousness of the offence, the person's age, past behaviour and ability to pay. The maximum fine a youth court can impose is £1000.
- absolute discharge – the offender is not penalized at all. It may be granted if the person was charged with a minor offence or the circumstances leading to the offence were beyond the person's control.
- conditional discharge – this may be granted if the offender undertakes not to re-offend during a set period of up to three years. If the person re-offends then he or she can be punished for both offences.

Parents of 16–17 year olds who have been convicted, can be bound over to look after their children properly – if they fail to do so they can be fined up to £1000. If the children are under 16, a parenting order is used to ensure that parents control their children. Failure to comply with a parenting order, which can include training for parents, will result in a fine of up to £1000.

Sentences for grievous bodily harm

For occasioning grievous bodily harm the court can apply any of the sentences given above or a custodial sentence. A youth court can give a custodial sentence of up to twelve months for two or more offences. Offenders can be detained for longer periods for first offences in very serious cases. If given a custodial sentence:

- 12–14 year olds will be admitted to a secure training centre
- 15–20 year olds will be admitted to a young offenders institution.

Activities

1. In groups of three you are to be the panel of magistrates considering this case. What do you consider to be the most appropriate sentence and why?
2. 'It's wrong to make someone suffer.' Discuss this statement in groups.
3. From a local court, the police or, using reference material in books or the Internet, find out the range of sentences for the following offences:
   - taking a car without the owner's consent
   - shoplifting
   - being drunk and disorderly.
4. What do you think of people who attack the elderly for the price of their pensions? Discuss in pairs.

Check it out

What you should have learned from this chapter

Look at the areas of study in the table. You should now know and understand the terminology and concepts that we have explored through Chapter 5: Criminal and civil law.

The activities and questions in the chapter, and the extra sheets your teacher will have worked through with you, should have helped you to learn about this topic.

If some of the areas are not clear, read through the pages again. If you are still not sure, ask your teacher to explain them again.

Area of study	Page
How does the law affect you?	79
Parents' duties	80
Consumers and the law	81
The law and discrimination	83
What is crime?	85
Law-making in action	87
European laws	89
I'll see you in court! (criminal and civil law)	89
People in the legal system	91
The rights of accused people	91

You should be able to answer all the following questions. These are short answer questions similar to those that will appear in Section A of the written exam paper that you will sit at the end of the course.

The knowledge and concepts covered in this chapter will also be tested in longer, more detailed questions in Sections B and D of the exam paper.

?

1. At what age can you have a job?
2. How old do you have to be to have a passport of your own?
3. Name three Acts of Parliament which are involved with consumer law.
4. List four different types of discrimination.
5. Where are police records stored?
6. Explain the term reprimand.
7. What is the difference between criminal and civil law?
8. List the stages of how a bill passes through Parliament and becomes a law.
9. What is the CPS?
10. What does a jury do?
11. Name three of the rights an accused person has.

6 The media

How much does the media influence our lives?

The media is one of the most pervasive and persuasive influences on life in the modern world. Television, radio, videos, magazines, newspapers, books, the Internet, advertisements and the cinema play an important role in the quality of life for many in Western society. We are exposed to the media in one form or another from an early age and it influences our thoughts, our attitudes and, in some cases, our behaviour. It has been estimated that the average Briton is exposed to 75 hours of media influence each week.

Freedom of Speech

The importance of the free communication of ideas and information cannot be over-emphasized. Article 19 of the United Nations Declaration of Human Rights states 'Everyone has the right to freedom of opinions and expression; this right includes freedom to hold opinions without interference and to seek, receive and impart information and ideas through the media, regardless of frontiers.'

Censorship

In some countries the news services are controlled by the state, which gives the controlling government, dictator or ruler an enormous amount of power. This may result in censorship of the press preventing any views that oppose those of the ruling power from being reported in the media. If the opposition view is reported, it is likely to be distorted or misrepresented.

Propaganda

Propaganda is the organized circulation of information designed to influence people. It usually attempts to appeal to people's emotions or prejudices, and it may contain huge distortions of the truth. Propaganda can be spread by many different media, although posters, leaflets, radio and the cinema are among the most widely used. Although mainly a wartime device, propaganda is used in peacetime by special interest groups, pressure groups or governments to make a point.

Spin doctors

A spin doctor is someone who tries to control the public response to an issue by presenting information in a particular way to the media. As the information has been manipulated and 'moved around' to promote one issue or aspect, to highlight a specific section or to minimize a contentious section, the story is said to have been given 'a spin'. Most spin doctors in the UK work in the political arena and most senior members of the government have spin doctors working for them. As they are not elected, they

Chinese propoganda poster (1966), showing Chairman Mao as the 'father of communism'

are independent of the electoral system and they are not publicly accountable for their actions. Spin doctors usually try to manipulate the media by:

- speaking to journalists off the record, i.e. without having their names mentioned in articles
- leaking information before a media story is released
- controlling the focus of attention in a news story
- selecting what news to release, when to release it and how to release it to the media.

Spin doctors control the amount of information given to the media at certain times so that they can create a 'slow news' day when they want to promote a particular policy or document. When they want to 'hide' a story, they will present other issues to the media to create a 'fast news' day. Spin doctors also work for large companies, charities and pressure groups.

Who owns the media?

The mass media refers to the system by which information and views on important and topical issues are conveyed to a huge number of people. The mass media includes television, radio, newspapers and magazines, and the Internet. The instrument through which information is delivered to the public, for example a particular newspaper or television programme, is known as a media outlet. More and more media outlets are being owned by fewer, larger companies and individuals. Individuals who own newspapers are known as press barons. Individuals who own media companies are known as media barons. An example is Rupert Murdoch, the head of News International which owns Sky Television, the *Sun*, the *Times* and other companies.

Who controls the media?

Some people argue that control of the international media is invested in a small number of powerful individuals and international news services from the developed world. They argue that there is an under-representation from less developed countries. Other people would argue that this system has set up its own checks over time and that it presents a balanced view of activities in the world today.

Rupert Murdoch – media baron

Fair reporting

Some people are concerned that only a few people and companies control such a large number of the world's media outlets. This is because the public rely on the media to provide information and the person who controls the transmission of that information can determine how the information is presented.

The media can be extremely influential in informing and moulding public opinion. The public must ensure that they consider each item of news and form their own opinion, rather than simply accepting the opinion transmitted by the media.

It is important that public information is given without bias so that people can form their own opinions. There is a danger that the media will be biased towards a particular belief or value system. As media companies get larger, the trend in media coverage becomes more global. The largest companies, for example the BBC, CNN and Associated Press, are based in the West, so reports tend to be biased towards Western ideals and values. This can be more exaggerated at times of national or international tension. In times of war the media tends to support the government and the nation's armed forces.

Monitoring the media

The operation of the media in the UK is monitored by two main bodies whose function is to control the standards of reporting information to the public. These bodies monitor television, advertising and press coverage of events.

The Press Complaints Commission (PCC) monitors the code of practice for publications. This code (originally published in January 1991) has been amended nearly thirty times. The Code of Practice Committee is made up of newspaper and magazine industy editors. If a newspaper is found guilty of contravening the code by the Press Complaints Commission it must print the commission's judgement in full and in a prominent position. Among others, the code covers the following issues:

- Publications must not print inaccurate, misleading or distorted materials.
- A fair opportunity for reply must be given to individuals or organizations.
- *Everyone is entitled to respect for his or her private life, home, health and correspondence.
- A person should not expect to be intimidated, harassed or pursued by journalists or photographers.
- *Children under sixteen should not be interviewed without an adult being present and without the consent of their parents. Pupils should not have their education disturbed and should not be photographed at school without the permission of the head teacher.
- *Children under the age of sixteen involved in sex cases must not be identified.
- The press must avoid identifying relatives or friends of persons convicted or accused of crime without their consent.
- Journalists should not obtain or seek to obtain information or pictures through misrepresentation or deception.
- Journalists must not identify victims of sexual assaults or publish material likely to result in such identification unless, by law, they are free to do so.
- The press must avoid prejudicial reference to a person's race, colour, religion, sex or sexual orientation, or to any physical or mental illness or disability.
- Journalists must not use financial information received for their own profit or gain.
- Journalists have a moral responsibility to protect confidential sources of information.
- Payment for articles must be made openly and through an agent or with a witness. Payments must not be made to convicted or confessed criminals or to their associates.

The 'paparazzi'

There may be exceptions to the clauses marked * where publication can be demonstrated to be in the public interest. The public interest includes:

- detecting and exposing crime or a serious misdemeanour
- protecting public health and safety
- preventing the public from being misled by some statement or action of an individual or organization.

The PCC will require a full explanation in any case where publication is claimed to be in the public interest. In the case of a child the editor would have to demonstrate exceptional public interest to override the interest of the child.

Television

Television viewing has become the main leisure activity for many families and elderly people in Britain. On an average day 38 million people in Britain will turn on the television and watch it for three hours. This means that the average Briton will spend eight years watching 'the box'. It is said that television:

- defines what we should think, what we should buy, what success is, what makes us happy, how we should behave
- removes people from the world outside the living room
- has reduced children's ability to create imaginative games. This view is supported by evidence from teachers
- influences children and can be their main educator. It is placed after parents aand before school as the learning influence for children
- can distort our view of reality if we are exposed to a daily diet of superficial, sensational, selfish, apathetic or violent people or situations; and
- concentrates on values based on wealth, power, physical beauty, strength.

Television is a strong and powerful tool in society. It should reinforce the best ideals and values.

The Internet

The Internet is a powerful tool in the transmission and accessing of information. It should be remembered that its use is largely based in the developed countries as computers are too expensive in many countries across the world. Although they rarely own their own computer, some people in LEDCs are able to use Internct cafes.

The easy access of information on the Internet causes concern with relation to national security, copyright law and the transmission of pornographic material. Individual rights could be jeopardized and the law may be broken. There is also a danger that some people may set up websites that transmit false information. Some people believe that censorship should be applied to the Internet, but any system would be costly to develop and difficult to operate.

An Internet café in India

Activities

1 Try to work out what your media consumption has been in the last week? Use all aspects of the media. Share you findings with a partner.

2 Find the same story in two different newspapers. Make notes on how the headlines, the pictures and words used change the slant of the story.

Are we influenced by advertising?

Advertising can be heard on the radio and seen on television, at the cinema, on billboards, on public transport and in newspapers and magazines. We can even find advertisements on the clothes we wear!

Manufacturers are prepared to spend large amounts of money to advertise their goods. Independent radio and television companies fund their programmes with income from advertising and sponsorship of programmes.

Some people think that advertising makes people buy things that they don't really want or need. Some people think that advertisements exaggerate the quality or range of their products and that humour and celebrity are used to encourage people to buy. Other people believe that advertisements have less influence than is made out and that, if there was no advertising, the general public would be less aware of the range of products available.

Who checks on advertisements?

Television advertising is regulated by the Independent Television Commission and radio advertising by the Radio Authority. These organizations are independent of the state, the advertisers and the broadcasting companies. Advertisements should be honest, decent and truthful. An advertising code sets out the rules for advertising on radio and television.

The code includes issues such as discrimination, decency and misrepresentation. Advertisements which do not take heed of the rules may be banned. The code has a specific section to cover advertisements which are meant for children. Advertisements 'must not include any material which might result in harm to them either physically, mentally or morally.'

A Activities

1. Find the names of five television programmes which are sponsored.
2. Choose any advertisement for an item of clothing. After a group discussion, make notes on who you think the advertisement is aimed at and whether it is successful.
3. Should firms be allowed to use personalities, for example footballers or pop stars, to promote their products?
4. Prepare an advertisement for a product. Who would you use to promote it and why?

Famous 'faces' sell products with sponsorship

Case study: The media

Three main types of newspaper are on sale in Britain today – national, provincial and local. National newspapers are sold across the country, provincial newspapers in a large area possibly covering a few counties, and local newspapers in a restricted local area. National and local newspapers differ in the type of news they include. Similarly, national newspapers differ in the choice of news items they carry and the way in which they present the same event.

Communication is the transmission of information. Newspapers transmit information through visual images (photographs) and written text (reports). The richness of language is often used to full effect in newspaper reports. As a word can have various meanings the careful choice of words can add a different focus to a story. The people involved in writing newspapers are well aware of the emotive or emotion-arousing power of language and use it to their best advantage. Newspaper editors know that they need to catch the reader's eye to encourage them to buy the paper.

What's in a headline?

A headline can be the most important part of a story. It attracts the reader's attention, sums up the story, stirs emotions or makes the reader want to find out the rest of the story. The headline helps to sell the paper.

SEARCH WARRANT

Police told: stop more suspects on the streets

Figure 6.1 From the *Daily Mirror*, 11 March 2002.

The headline in Figure 6.1 is a play on the words 'search warrant'. We all recognize that a search warrant is the name of a legal document giving the police permission to search a property. Giving people warrant means giving permission. So the title is giving police permission to search people. The standfirst (the print below the headline which explains the main headline) explains what the police are expected to do under their new powers.

Using photographs and captions

Photographs are used to attract readers to buy the paper. Journalists try to ensure that they have a good photograph to back up their story. Captions are used to explain the meaning or the context of the photograph. By changing the focus of the caption attached to a photograph, it is possible to channel readers' thoughts to different issues.

The photograph and caption below supported the headline in Figure 6.1. The article is about new powers for police in the stop and search procedure. If the caption is changed to 'Police criticized for use of force when searching', a different focus is given to the article.

From the *Daily Mirror*, 11 March 2002

POWERS: Police search a suspect

Facts and opinions

Every article printed in a newspaper will contain one or both of the following styles of writing:

- facts. A fact is something which can be proved to be true. All news stories have to be factually correct. They should answer the questions: Who? What? Where? When? Why?
- opinions. These are the views of the writer and are usually found on the letter pages, and in reviews and editorials. Sometimes it is difficult to tell opinion from fact as opinions can be disguised as facts. They can give very little or misleading information and are often written as if they are facts, for example:
  - Digital television is the greatest technological achievement of the twentieth century.
  - Robbie Williams is the best male singer ever.

The editorial in Figure 6.2 was printed before the article in Figure 6.3. While there are some facts in this editorial, it is based on the editor's opinion and feeling about the situation.

Comparing newspaper reports

The two newspaper reports in Figure 6.3 and 6.4 cover the same story – discussions which took place between British Prime Minister Tony Blair and other European leaders at the European Summit in Barcelona, Spain, during the weekend of 15–17 March 2002. One article appeared in the *Mirror* and the other in the *Guardian*. Both articles appeared on Saturday 16 March 2002.

You should read the two newspaper reports carefully at least twice. In order to compare the two articles you need to think about what aspects are the same and what are different. You should note down:

- facts which are in both articles (perhaps five)
- facts that are in one article but not in the other
- how the headline is used
- how the picture and caption are used, if appropriate.

VOICE OF THE Mirror

Don't play Saddam's mad game

SADDAM Hussein would be mad to take on the might of America. But of course that is exactly what he is.

He swaggeringly revels in once again becoming the focus of international debate.

He sees America preparing to launch an attack on Iraq and positively enjoys the prospect.

Like a bar-room brawler, he sneers at President Bush the equivalent of: 'Come on, big boy, let's see how tough you are.'

Saddam believes he cannot lose. He will either force the US to back down or suffer such terrible destruction of his country that Arab sympathy will be with him.

This is not a question of who is right and who is wrong. Saddam Hussein is an evil despot who crushes his own people and threatens the world.

But that does not mean an all-out military assault against him is the right way forward.

Mr Bush should listen to Jordan's King Abdullah. Yesterday he warned that an attack on Iraq would undermine the war on terrorism and destabilise the Middle East.

Saddam needs to be neutralised and controlled. Not made stronger.

Figure 6.2 From the *Daily Mirror*, 13 March 2002

BLOODY DANGEROUS

EU's fear on Iraq attack

By JAMES HARDY

EUROPE yesterday told Tony Blair that an all-out assault on Iraq could threaten world peace.

As riot police clashed with thousands of anti-globalisation protesters outside the EU summit, it was made clear to the PM that any strikes against Saddam Hussein must have the full backing of the United Nations.

And Germany said it would only help fight a war against Iraq if it was backed by a UN mandate.

Mr Blair has used the EU summit in Spain to try to rally support from the other 14 countries.

But the resounding message was that the US and Britain must not go it alone – and military action must be a last resort.

Foreign Secretary Jack Straw put a brave face on the rebuff, insisting: 'The whole world has made a decision that Iraq poses a very serious threat to the international community.'

He added that the US had already stressed any decisions had to be 'talked over carefully'.

German leader Gerhard Schroeder accused the UK of putting relations with the US before its place in Europe. Although German forces currently in Kuwait would 'help out' if needed, he said only UN backing would see him send troops to Iraq.

Throughout the debate in Barcelona, running battles between police and protesters raged outside. Bottles and stones were thrown by the rioters, many of whom wore masks.

Bins were set alight and blazing tyres thrown on a train line.

More than 8 500 police have been drafted in from across Spain.

Briton Guy Taylor said the officers provoked the riot. He said: 'Police hit out with batons.'

Figure 6.3 From the *Daily Mirror*, 16 March 2002

The *Mirror* headline

The headline is large and heavy and uses emotive and ambiguous language, in particular the word 'bloody'. This report was on page 2 of the paper. The headline above this was 'Bloody Stupid'. The double use of the adjective catches the attention. The headline could refer to a possible attack on Iraq. Equally, it could refer to the battle between police and protestors. The standfirst indicates that the story is about the EU Summit, but the picture and caption support the story being about police and protestors.

Five facts in the *Mirror* article

- The message from the EU is that Britain and the US must not go it alone.
- Police clash with anti-globalization protestors.
- Description of 'riots' taking place.
- More than 8500 police officers have been drafted from across Spain.
- Fighter jets, anti-aircraft missiles and warships were on hand to counter terrorist attacks.
- Fighter jets, anti-aircraft missiles and warships were on standby to counter terrorist attacks.

Blair woos summit amid fears of split

Ian Black in Barcelona

There was mounting nervousness over the potential of the Iraq issue to cause divisions within the EU when Tony Blair canvassed the mood of his colleagues at the Barcelona summit last night.

Turkey, a key member of Nato, warned against any attack, arguing that Iraq did not constitute a threat to its neighbours. 'We feel that Iraq should not be the subject of military attacks because it would upset the whole Middle East,' the prime minister Bulent Ecevit told reporters after meeting EU leaders.

Mr Blair discussed the looming crisis with Gerhard Schröder, the German chancellor, but made clear that no decision had been made on specific measures to be taken against the Iraqi president. 'We are not at the stage of decisions,' the prime minister insisted.

Belgium, which this week proposed sending a high-level EU mission to Baghdad, was preparing a statement to be issued when the summit ends today.

Formally, the EU has no policy on Iraq because of sharp disagreements between Britain and France: but all 15 members are urging Baghdad to abide by UN security council disarmament resolutions.

Jack Straw, the foreign secretary, kept up the drumbeat, emphasising agreement on the threat so far and sidestepping evident divisions about the way ahead. 'The whole world has made a decision that Iraq poses a very serious threat to the security of the region and to the security of the international community,' he said.

It has not escaped the notice of his co-summiteers that Mr Blair was the only EU leader visited by US vice-president Dick Cheney this week.

EU members hope pressure on Saddam will oblige him to bow to demands that he readmit UN weapons inspectors.

'If there is military action it will not take place in 24 hours,' the EU's foreign policy chief, Javier Solana, told the BBC. 'We will have plenty of time. We want to see how the situation may evolve in New York and the United Nations.'

Figure 6.4 From the *Guardian*, 16 March 2002

The *Guardian* headline

The *Guardian* article was placed among regular and routine reports in the national news section on page 16. It was not attempting to be emotional or dramatic so the headline is a description of events, if somewhat enhanced to catch the interest by the use of the words woo and fear.

Five facts in the *Guardian* article

- Turkey warned against attacking Iraq.
- EU stress that Iraq should be urged to abide by UN Security Council disarmament resolutions.
- Belgium suggested an EU mission to Baghdad.
- Mr Cheney, the US vice-president, visited Tony Blair this week.
- Quote from EU foreign policy spokesman that military action against Iraq is not imminent.

Five common facts

- The discussions took place in Barcelona.
- Tony Blair and German leader Gerhard Schröder were involved in discussion.
- Other EU states will not act without the full sanction of the UN.
- Both quote British Foreign Secretary Jack Straw though one quote has been edited.
- Any attack on Iraq could threaten world peace or cause EU division.

A Activities

1. In pairs, study the editorial in Figure 6.8 and highlight all emotive, persuasive or dramatic language used. Do you think the editorial is designed to inform, shock, persuade or advise? Why do you think this?
2. Suggest two different headlines for the story about police stop and search powers (Figure 6.1) and two different captions for the photograph (page 102). Make notes of your suggestions.
3. Do you prefer the style of the *Mirror* article (Figure 6.3) or the *Guardian* article (Figure 6.4)? Why?

Check it out

What you should have learned from this chapter

Look at the areas of study in the table. You should now know and understand the terminology and concepts that we have explored in Chapter 6: The media.

The activities and questions in the chapter, and the worksheets your teacher will have worked through with you, should have helped you to learn about this topic.

If some of the areas are not clear, read through the pages again. If you are still not sure ask your teacher to explain them again.

Area of study	Page
What is freedom of speech?	97
Who controls the media	98
What is fair reporting?	98
How the media is monitored	99
Television	100
The Internet	100
How we are influenced by advertising in the press and on television	101
How is advertising regulated?	101

You should be able to answer all the following questions. These are short answer questions similar to those that will appear in Section A of the written exam paper that you will sit at the end of the course.

The knowledge and concepts covered in this chapter will also be tested in longer, more detailed questions in Sections B and D of the exam paper.

?

1. What do we mean by the term the media?
2. Name one media baron.
3. List five daily newspapers.
4. Name a British news company.
5. Name a foreign news company.
6. What organization is responsible for monitoring publications?
7. Who controls advertising?
8. Define the term freedom of speech.
9. Explain what is meant by censorship.
10. Name three effects that people say television has on our lives.

Global citizenship

Key ideas

Chapter 7 International relations

* The Commonwealth and the United Nations
* The UK and NATO

Chapter 8 World trade and overseas aid

* Global inequality
* Sustainable development

Chapter 9 Exploring global issues

* Poverty
* Finance
* Human rights abuses
* The issue of arms and weapons
* Global warming
* Acid rain
* Deforestation
* Protecting the world's ecosystems
* What are you doing to do about it?

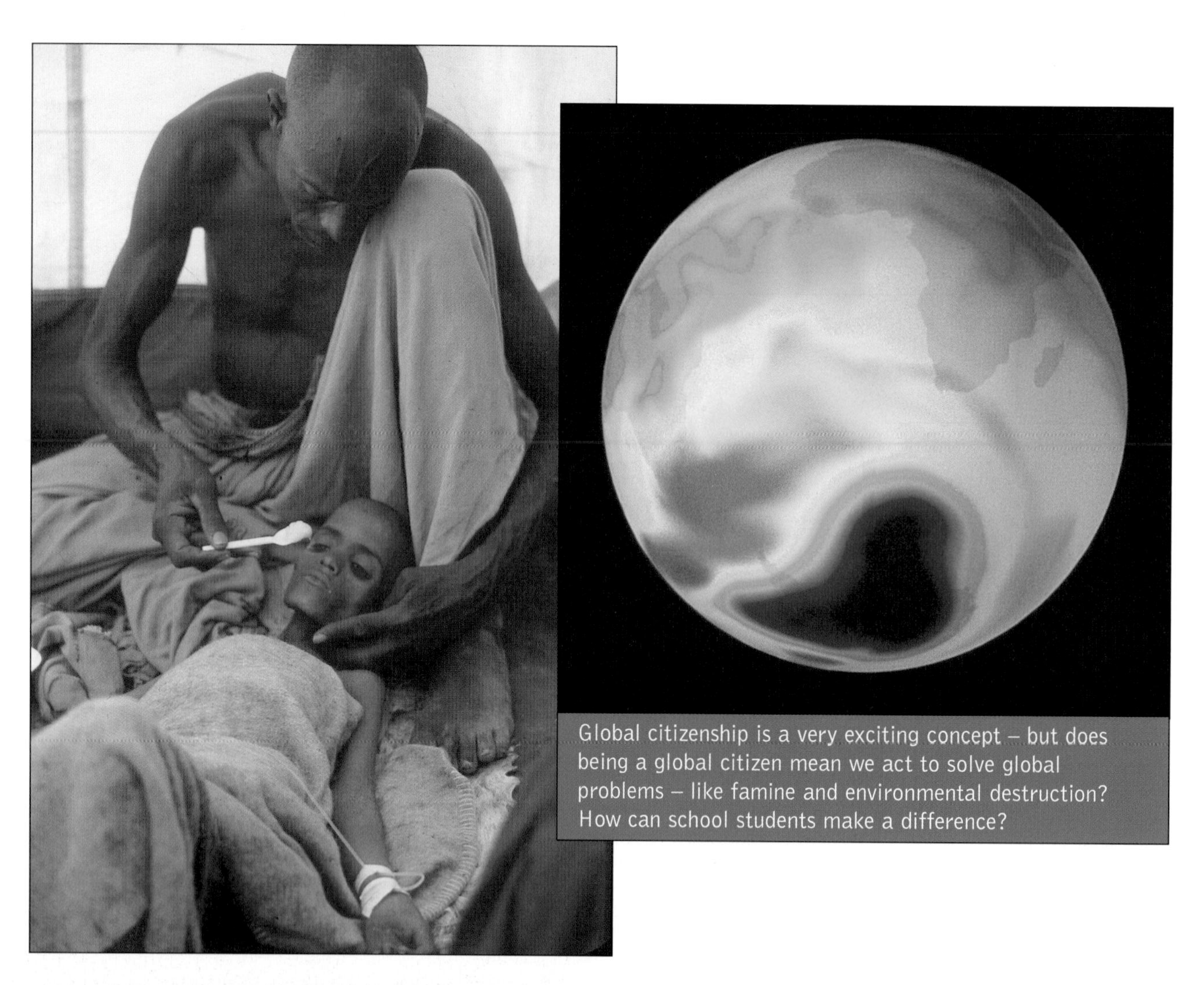

Global citizenship is a very exciting concept – but does being a global citizen mean we act to solve global problems – like famine and environmental destruction? How can school students make a difference?

What can we do to make sure we communicate **without** using force?

7 International relations

The Commonwealth and the United Nations

Sometimes countries are referred to as nation states. For centuries, the nation state was central to international relations across the world. This was because each country controlled its own goods and services so the economy of one country remained distinct from the economy of another country. As world trade has increased, businesses across the world have become larger and communication has become easier, the world economy has become more global. This has made it much easier for countries to co-operate and share experiences and trade with each other. The growth of large companies and multinationals has led to the decline of the nation state as a single entity and has promoted membership of groups of nations with common aims and aspirations.

The UK's relationship with the Commonwealth and the UN

As a member of the EU, the Commonwealth and the UN, the UK often has to tread a careful diplomatic path so it does not damage its relationships with one or other of these organizations. The UK's position with respect to trading practices as part of the EU could conflict with long-standing trading agreements with Commonwealth countries. Similarly, the UK may be a party to a decision of the Commonwealth countries which has not been agreed by the UN. This diplomatic role is undertaken on behalf of the country by the Foreign Office and the UK is often represented at meetings of the EU, Commonwealth and UN by the Foreign Secretary.

The Commonwealth

The nations and dependencies which were formerly the British Empire are now linked together in an organization called the Commonwealth. The Commonwealth was created by an Act of Parliament in 1931 and currently consists of 54 sovereign nations and dependencies. Canada, Australia, New Zealand and the UK have remained Commonwealth partners since 1931. South Africa joined in 1931, left in 1961 and rejoined in 1994.

Heads of State from Commonwealth countries meet every two years for a conference. Every four years the athletes from Commonwealth countries compete in the Commonwealth Games. In 2002 these games were held in Manchester.

The Commonwealth conference

The Commonwealth supports free trade between member countries. Some people believe that this loose association of countries looks back to the time when Britain had an empire and exploited the people and resources of its colonies. Other people are proud of Britain's past and its ongoing relationship with this group of nations around the world.

Activities

1 Find out the aims of the Commonwealth. To what extent are these aims met by this confederation of nations?

2 What advantages and disadvantages can you think of for the UK's continued membership of the Commonwealth?

3 Do you think Britain owes anything to her former colonies?

The aims of the United Nations

The United Nations (UN), which was established after World War II, aims to promote international peace, security and co-operation. The UK was one of the founder members. The United Nations Assembly is made up of representatives of each of the 185 member countries. Each country has one vote. Resolutions are discussed by the assembly and they often become the basis for creating international law. A UN resolution is held in high esteem in most countries of the world.

Each member country must contribute a minimum of 0.1 per cent of the UN budget, which must be paid in US dollars. This method of financing the UN causes problems for countries with weak economies as their currencies are often devalued and worthless against the dollar. Powerful countries, like the USA, have often withheld their contribution to the UN for a variety of reasons. This has led to the cancellation of some UN projects.

Membership of the UN requires member states to sign the United Nations Charter, which commits member states to supporting the aims and objectives of the UN. These include:

- the maintenance of international peace and security
- arms control
- the protection of human rights
- the giving of aid to refugees and famine victims.

The UN has prepared guidelines and laws which govern the operation of its aims and objectives.

The UN building in New York

How is the UN organized?

The UN is governed by a charter together with a series of commission statements and defining articles relating to procedure and practice.

UN peacekeeping forces

One of the roles undertaken by the UK for the UN is that of peacekeeper (Figure 7.3). At times of conflict or disorder in a country, such as in Bosnia, Sierra Leone or Afghanistan, the UN asks member states if they will provide defence troops from their armed forces to form a peacekeeping force in the country. The UK held a unique position in Afghanistan. Together with the USA, the UK was involved in a campaign to remove terrorist personnel from Afghanistan after the suicide attacks on the World Trade Center on 11 September 2001. At the same time a further 2000 British troops were part of the 4800-strong international force which the UN placed in Afghanistan to support the new government and keep peace in the country during the period of rebuilding and reconciliation after the removal of the Taliban regime.

Being part of a peacekeeping force is not without its cost. During a period of five years 60 British service personnel lost their lives undertaking peacekeeping duties in the Balkans, Sierra Leone and Afghanistan.

A UN peacekeeping force in action

The UN Secretariat is based in New York and is headed by the Secretary-General of the United Nations. The Secretary-General is elected by the General Assembly and is responsible for running the UN.

The UN General Assembly meets annually and is made up of representatives of the 185 members of the UN. The developing nations outnumber the developed nations by three to one on this council. For a decision to be made a two-thirds majority is required so it is often difficult to reach an agreement.

The UN Security Council was set up after World War II. The council has five permanent members – the UK, China, France, Russia and the USA – and ten temporary members. The five permanent members have the right to veto any decision. Resolutions are passed by a majority vote unless the right to veto has been used. The Security Council's job is to discuss threats to international security, to suggest solutions or propose action. Action could include trade sanctions or the removal of aid to a country. As a last resort, the option of military intervention is available. The Security Council deals with issues relating to the arms trade and weapons of mass destruction as well as dealing with UN peacekeeping forces.

The UN Environment Programme (UNEP)

The UNEP was set up to review the global environment. It is responsible to the UN for safeguarding the global environment for future generations. The UNEP is based in Nairobi, Kenya. One of its projects monitors the types and numbers of different plant and animal species found in different parts of the world. The UNEP has the power to name protected species and to create protected areas for them.

In addition, this programme deals with research into the effect global warming and acid rain will have on the environment. Action on global warming was agreed at the UN Conference on Environment and Development that was held in Rio de Janeiro in 1992 (Figure 7.4). Countries agreed to implement UNEP Agenda 21 – a plan of action to improve the environment which should be implemented locally, nationally and globally.

A conference held in Kyoto, Japan, in 1999 showed that many of the proposed and agreed environmental developments had not been implemented. The conference reports are evidence that the UN cannot force member countries to implement the decisions made at the UN or any international conferences it holds.

UN Commission on Human Rights

The UN Universal Declaration of Human Rights led to the creation of a UN commission to monitor its operation. The commission monitors countries for human rights abuses such as torture or discrimination, reports human rights abuses to the UN General Assembly and liaises with governments and other groups to improve human rights across the world. It is helped in its work by non-governmental organizations (NGOs) such as Amnesty International.

The Earth Summit at Rio (1992)

Activities

1 Should the UN have more power to make governments keep to environmental targets? Discuss.
2 Find out what Article 2 of the UN Declaration of Human Rights states. Why is it important?
3 In pairs, look at a daily national newspaper. Can you find any evidence of human rights abuses?
4 How important are NGOs in fighting human rights abuses? Discuss in groups.

Flags of the countries in the UN

The UK and NATO

The North Atlantic Treaty was signed in Washington on 4 April 1949 creating the North Atlantic Treaty Organization (NATO), an alliance of twelve independent nations including the UK committed to each other's defence. Four further European nations joined the organization between 1952 and 1982. On 12 March 1999 the Czech Republic, Hungary and Poland joined the alliance to bring the total number of members to nineteen.

NATO created the North Atlantic Co-operation Council in 1991, the Partnership for Peace in 1994 and the Euro-Atlantic Partnership Council in 1997 to open new forms of partnership and co-operation with other nations, particularly Mediterranean and east European countries. As a result of this spirit of co-operation the alliance signed an agreement on future relations with Russia on 27 May 1997. Discussions are taking place on the possibility of further countries joining the alliance and on changes to the structure and procedures of NATO.

NATO has a fundamental role to safeguard the freedom and security of its member countries. Its first task is to deter and defend against any threat of aggression to any member country. In order to achieve this, NATO plays a key role in the field of crisis management by contributing to conflict prevention and, where appropriate, taking action to resolve any crisis. The alliance is committed to promoting partnership and co-operation with other countries in the Euro-Atlantic area aimed at increasing

The nineteen member countries of NATO are:

Belgium	UK
Canada	USA
Denmark	Germany
France	Greece
Iceland	Spain
Italy	Turkey
Luxembourg	Czech Republic
Netherlands	Hungary
Norway	Poland
Portugal	

NATO forces on exercise

mutual confidence and the capacity for joint action. As part of this co-operation, NATO was actively involved in the implementation of the 1995 Dayton Peace Agreement on Bosnia and Herzegovina. It established and led a multinational force to help build the basis for future peace in the region. Similarly, it leads a multinational force in Kosovo aimed at reversing the ethnic cleansing in the country to enable thousands of Kosovar refugees, who fled from the repression in 1999, to return safely to their homeland. It is hoped that NATO involvement in Kosovo will allow people to live together in peace regardless of their ethnic origins, will help them rebuild their homes and lives, and will create a strong, democratic society and a lasting peace.

To enable it to meet its objectives, the alliance has established a sense of political solidarity and military co-operation over the last fifty years. Member countries meet regularly to discuss issues of joint interest and concern and to plan future areas of co-operation. The armed forces of the member countries, including those of the UK, join together to undertake planned military exercises. This builds trust, confidence and understanding to enable these separate military units to work together should a crisis or conflict arise.

Activities

1 Which members of NATO are members of the EU?

2 Should any country be able to join NATO? Form small groups in your class and discuss.

3 Is NATO necessary? Discuss in pairs.

Case study: International conflict – Iraq

Events leading to the Gulf War

Iraq's invasion and annexation of Kuwait took place on 2 August 1990, two years after the end of the Iran–Iraq war which had left Iraq politically bruised and in debt. Iraq owed £70 billion, half of which was owed to the Gulf states, mainly Kuwait (Figure 7.1). Saddam Hussein, President of Iraq, accused the Arab League Summit held in May 1990 of maintaining low oil prices to harm his country. He said that members of the Arab League were waging 'economic war' on Iraq. In July, the Iraqi foreign minister, Tariq Aziz, accused Kuwait of stealing £1.3 billion of Iraqi oil from the neutral zone and he wrote off £5.5 billion of Kuwaiti loans to Iraq.

Towards the end of July, the world was faced with a Middle East crisis when 30 000 Iraqi troops moved to the Kuwaiti border. Egyptian President Hosni Mubarak attempted to mediate. US Ambassador to Iraq, April Glaspie, warned Iraq that the USA would use its powers to protect its friends in the Gulf. On 27 July, Kuwait agreed to Iraq's demands for compensation but refused to give up the islands of Bubiyan and Warba to Iraq. By this time, Iraq had 100 000 troops on the Kuwaiti border. It took only one day for Iraq to take full possession of Kuwait.

The UN Security Council was called to an emergency session and an emergency meeting of Arab League foreign ministers was held in Cairo. The UN imposed economic sanctions to be effective immediately and declared Iraq's annexation of Kuwait as null and void. The UN set a deadline of 15 January 1991 for the Iraqi withdrawal from Kuwait.

As the deadline for withdrawal approached, UN-controlled forces began to mass in the Gulf area. The force included naval vessels and air attack equipment in addition to tanks and other armoured fighting vehicles. Naval vessels were summoned to form a blockade on Iraq. Warships came from Australia, Britain, Canada, Holland, France, Italy and the USA. Despite warnings from the UN and governments across the world, Iraq did not withdraw. On Wednesday 16 January 1991, the war began.

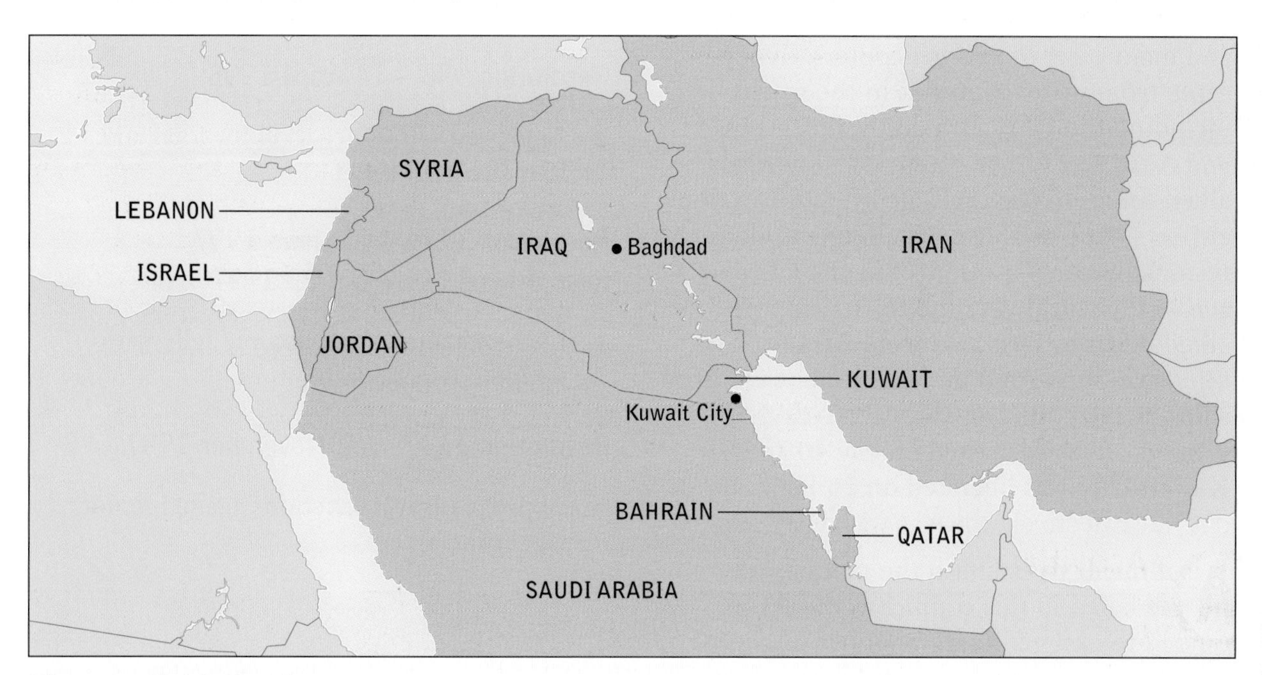

Figure 7.1 The Gulf region

US soldiers in the Gulf War

The Gulf War

The Gulf War, Operation Desert Storm, lasted 44 days from 16 January until 28 February 1991. During this time allied forces, including the USA and Britain, fought to ensure the implementation of UN resolutions. The allied forces, commanded by American General Norman Schwarzkopf, were supported with heavy artillery including tanks and other armoured vehicles, warships and many aircraft and helicopters. Troops came from many countries in the world including the USA, Britain, France, Canada and Australia. Other countries allowed the allied forces to use their facilities, for example airports were used for refuelling and docks for restocking ships. Countries in the EU and across the world gave money to support the allied effort to oust Iraq from Kuwait. The air offensive, supported by missile launches from ships in the Gulf, lasted for forty days. The ground offensive started on day 40 and Kuwait City was liberated on 26 February – day 42. Effectively the war was over.

It is difficult to establish the number of people killed in this conflict as the Iraqis tended to exaggerate the number of people killed and injured while the allies tried to minimize the numbers. The death toll was only part of the human cost of the war to the people of Iraq.

UN Resolutions

Resolution 660 – 2 August 1990

- Condemned invasion of Kuwait
- Demanded Iraq's withdrawal and called on both countries to begin negotiations

Resolution 661 – 6 August 1990

- Imposed trade and financial embargo on Iraq and occupied Kuwait
- Established special sanctions committee to implement resolution
- Called upon UN members to protect assets of Kuwait around the world

Resolution 687 – 3 April 1991

- Formally ended Gulf War
- Authorized inspection and elimination of Iraq's suspected weapons of mass destruction

Resolution 986 – 14 April 1995

- Approved sale of Iraqi oil for food and humanitarian relief

Resolution 1115 – 21 June 1997
Resolution 1134 – Oct 23 1997

- Demanded that Iraq comply fully with weapon inspection regimes

Resolution 1137 – 12 November 1997

- Approved travel sanctions against senior Iraqi officials

Continuing conflict

Since the end of the Gulf War in 1991, the continued conflict between the USA and Iraq has erupted several times into violence. Tension between the USA and Iraq started to build up again after the bombing of the World Trade Center in New York on 11 September 2001.

The causes

The main cause of the continued hostility between the USA and Iraq is disagreement over the extent and need for continued UN inspections. The US and the UN claim that Iraq is not abiding by the terms of the agreement made at the end of the Gulf War but is continuing to develop weapons of mass destruction. Iraq denies these claims and says that the USA is trying to undermine its national sovereignty and cripple the country through continued economic sanctions.

Another point of contention is the continuation of 'no-fly zones' over northern and southern Iraq. These were originally designed to protect the Kurdish minority in the north and the Shiite minority in the south. These zones are Iraqi airspace in which Iraqi planes are not allowed to fly. The hostility was heightened when Iraq refused to recognize the validity of the 'no-fly-zones' in 1998.

The wreckage in Kuwait after the Gulf War

Iraq maintains that it is being punished unfairly by the USA. The USA maintains that Saddam Hussein and his government are responsible for the continuing action against Iraq because Iraq has failed to comply with the UN resolutions relating to its post-Gulf War responsibilities.

After the attacks in New York in September 2001, the USA turned its efforts to combating terrorism across the world. George W Bush, the American President, stated that every effort would be made to remove the terrorists and that the countries who helped them, including Iraq, would be punished.

Bomb damage in Baghdad

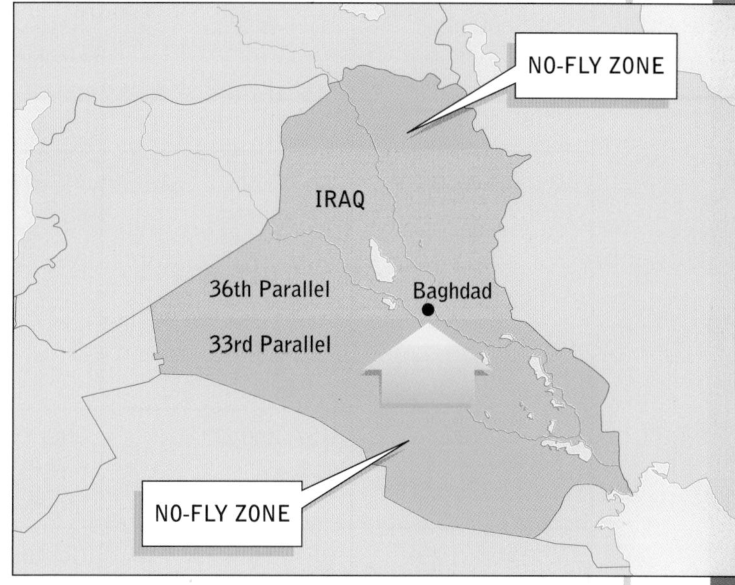

Figure 7.2 Map of 'no-fly zones' in Iraq (1992 Magellan Geographix, Santa Barbara, CA)

Date	Countries involved	Type of action	Details of action
2 August 1992	USA and UN vs Iraq	Establishment of 'no-fly' zone	No-fly zone imposed over south attacks on rebels. USA begins air patrols of the zone.
28 December 1992	USA vs Iraq	Air combat to enforce 'no-fly' zone	US plane shoots down Iraqi Mig-25 when it enters the 'no-fly' zone.
13 January 1993	USA, UK and France vs Iraq	Retaliatory air and missile strike	Gulf coalition forces strike Iraqi radar and missile sites.
17 January 1993	USA vs Iraq	Retaliatory missile strike	USA strike nuclear facility outside Baghdad to punish Iraq for non-compliance with UN weapons inspections.
27 June 1993	USA vs Iraq	Retaliatory missile strike	USA fires 24 missiles from ships at intelligence headquarters in Baghdad to stop alleged plot to assassinate former President Bush.
7 October 1994	USA and Kuwait vs Iraq	Military build-up to a renewed crisis	US planes and 54 000 troops head for the Gulf as Iraq's troops prepare to attack Kuwait. Iraq pulls back its army.
31 August 1996	Iraq and KDP (Kurdistan Democratic Party) vs PUK (Patriotic Union of Kurdistan)	Iraq helps one faction in Kurdish civil war	Iraq seizes city of Irbil inside the Kurdish 'protected area' in northern Iraq, which is protected by US-led troops.
3–4 September 1996	USA vs Iraq	Retaliatory missile strikes	USA fires missiles at Iraqi military targets. US President Clinton extends 'no-fly' zones to cover parts of Baghdad and central Iraq.
16–20 December 1998	USA and UK vs Iraq	Retaliatory missile strike	Operation Desert Fox – attacks on sites relating to production of nuclear, chemical and biological weapons in retaliation for failing to co-operate with UN inspections. As a result, Iraq said it would end all inspections and militarily challenge the 'no-fly' zones.
29–30 December 1998	USA and UK vs Iraq	Iraq fires missiles on US aircraft in 'no-fly' zone	Allied forces respond and destroy Iraqi defence battery.
December 1998 –present	USA and UK vs Iraq	Continued missile attacks	Allied forces continue to enforce UN line in Iraq.

Figure 7.3 Iraq – the continuing conflict

The effects of sanctions

UNICEF and other UN bodies agree that the sanctions have had a terrible toll on the people of Iraq (Figures 7.4 and 7.5). It is estimated that up to 1 million people have died from starvation and disease in the last ten years. However, it appears that sanctions have not had the required effect on Saddam Hussein who has often used the situation for political advantage. Some would argue that sanctions have strengthened his position in Iraq.

Christian Aid's experience of sanctions

The immediate consequence of eight years of sanctions has been a dramatic fall in living standards, the collapse of the infrastructure, and a serious decline in the availability of public services. The long-term damage to the fabric of society has yet to be assessed but economic disruption has already led to heightened levels of crime, corruption and violence.

Figure 7.4 From *Working in Iraq: Christian Aid's Experience 1990–1998*, Christian Aid

Squeezed to death

The change in 10 years is unparalleled in my experience. In 1989, the literacy rate was 95%; and 93% of the population had free access to modern health facilities. Parents were fined for failing to send their children to school. The phenomenon of children begging was unheard of. Iraq had reached a stage where the basic indicators we use to measure the overall well-being of human beings, including children, were some of the best in the world. Now it is in the bottom 20%. **In 10 years, child mortality has gone from one of the lowest in the world to one of the highest.**

Figure 7.5 John Pilger quotes UNICEF's senior representative in Iraq, Anapama Rao Singh, from the *Guardian*, 4 March 2000

Saddam Hussein among his followers

A Activities

1. Look at the photos on pages 116–119 carefully. Choose one and describe it in detail. What are your impressions as you look at the photo?
2. Are the UN and the US right to continue with sanctions in Iraq? Discuss in groups. Make notes of the views expressed.
3. How does the UN continue to control the 'no-fly zones'? Use Figure 7.2 to help with this. Is it right to do so?
4. What do you think needs to be done to resolve this conflict? Discuss in pairs.

Check it out

What you should have learned from this chapter

Look at the areas of study in the table. You should now know and understand the terminology and concepts that we have explored in Chapter 7: International relations.

The activities and questions in the chapter, and the worksheets your teacher will have worked through with you, should have helped you to learn about this topic.

If some of the areas are not clear, read through the pages again. If you are still not sure ask your teacher to explain them again.

Area of study	Page
What is the Commonwealth?	109
The aims of the United Nations	110
How the UN is organized	111
The UN Security Council	111
The role of UN peacekeeping forces	111
UN commission on Human Rights	112
The role of NATO	113

You should be able to answer all the following questions. These are short answer questions similar to those that will appear in Section A of the written exam paper that you will sit at the end of the course.

The knowledge and concepts covered in this chapter will also be tested in longer, more detailed questions in Section B and D of the exam paper.

?

1 What is the Commonwealth? When was the Commonwealth created?

2 How many countries belong to the Commonwealth?

3 What does UN stand for?

4 When was the UN created? How many countries belong to it?

5 Briefly explain what the Security Council does and who its members are.

6 Name three countries in which UN peacekeeping forces have operated.

7 Give an example of a project carried out by the UNEP.

8 What is the role of the UN Commission on Human Rights?

9 Name five members of NATO?

10 What is the main role of NATO?

8 World trade and overseas aid

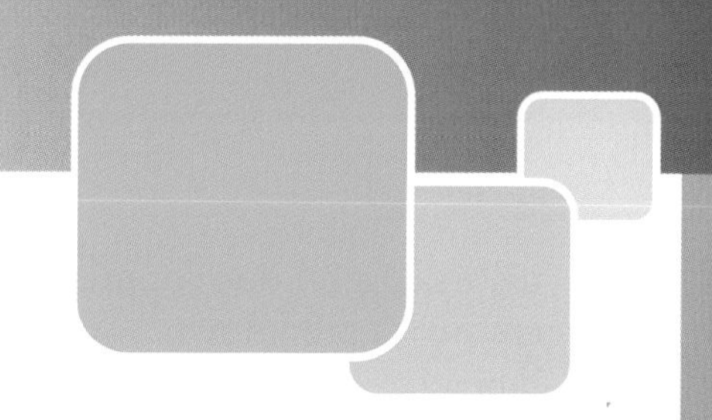

Global inequality

The development gap

Figure 8.1 shows the distribution of wealth in the world in 1981 when the Brandt Commission reported its findings on world development. In simple terms, the world is divided into two halves – the wealthy North and the poorer South. This is known as the North–South divide. The main finding of this report was that two-thirds of the world's population lived in poverty while the remaining third enjoyed a large proportion of the world's wealth. This is known as the 'development gap'.

To move away from this division into a rich and poor world, the United Nations now classifies the world's 206 nations into 'high income', 'middle income' and 'low income' countries. The 'high income' countries include the USA, Canada, Australia, Japan and most of Western Europe. These countries hold a disproportionate share of the world's wealth, trade investment, use of resources and access to information. The 'middle income' countries include much of Latin America, the Middle East, Eastern Europe and individual countries in north and south Africa. The 'low income' countries mostly lie south of the equator. Their citizens live in poor conditions and many die from disease or hunger. The gaps are still there.

Developed countries (MEDCs)

The most powerful countries in the world are those which are rich through having a developed economy. Many of these countries are in Western Europe. Together with North America and other developed countries they have shared aspirations and social and political values. They have become known as the West. These countries have undergone industrial and social change together with economic and

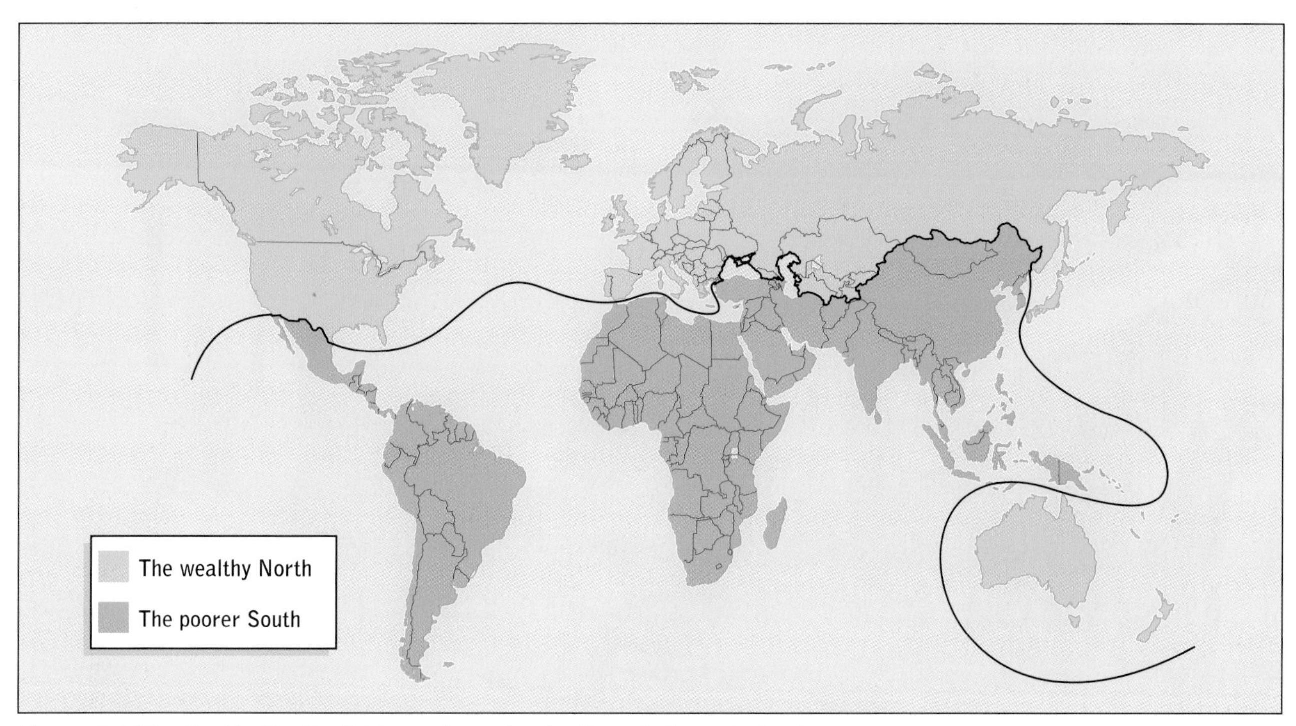

Figure 8.1 The North–South divide as shown by the Brandt Commission in 1981

technological development. Developed countries are known as First World countries. They have low death rates, low birth rates, low infant mortality and high life expectancy. These countries have a highly developed infrastructure including transport, communications, public health systems and public hygiene services. They are also known as More Economically Developed Countries (MEDCs).

Developing countries (LEDCs)

Countries with a less developed infrastructure and which are not yet fully industrialized are known as developing countries. These countries are often described as Third World countries. They have a lower standard of living than a developed country. It is usual to find high death rates and high birth rates with higher infant mortality and lower life expectancy than in developed countries. Life in developing countries is made more difficult because the economic gap between the First World and the Third World is increasing. The problem is worsening because many countries in the Third World have amassed considerable debts which they are finding difficult to repay. Basic services suffer as a result. The countries which still require major developments are known as Less Economically Developed Countries (LEDCs).

History will show that the Third World countries have not always been poor. Changes took place when European settlers, including the British, French and Spanish, sought land overseas with the aim of extending their economic and political power. They explored, invaded and took control of vast areas of the world. Colonialism explains how and why the development gap has emerged. It weakened the local economy through the removal of valuable physical resources and devastated communities as millions of young men and women were taken as slaves.

Although these countries now have independence, most African states are still dependent upon European countries for trade and finance. In South Africa, apartheid ended in 1994, but there is much inequality in the country and the white population is still the wealthiest. In Zimbabwe, land reform has led to conflict and loss of life. This issue is not yet resolved.

The poverty gap between rich and poor widens

Who holds power?

People and organizations that have power can make individuals, groups of individuals or whole countries do what they want them to do. Sometimes coercion is used which means making people do something they don't want to do. To study citizenship, you need to understan d the types of power and their uses (see Figure 8.2). As countries and world trade develop, a process of interdependence, or globalization, has emerged. As a result, power can be wielded on a global scale.

Activities

1. Do you think the countries that colonized parts of the world have a moral responsibility to the poorer nations they colonized? Discuss in groups.
2. Make a list of the differences between developing and developed countries.
3. Discuss why you think that power is concentrated in the developed countries.
4. Should Britain write off the debt owed by the world's poorest nations? Discuss in groups.

Closing the development gap

Closing the development gap cannot be a short-term challenge, nor will it be easy. The export of raw materials is often the only source of income in a developing country. The raw materials are sold cheaply and the economy of the country is dependent on that income. Consequently very few LEDCs have developed manufacturing industries. Prices for world commodities are subject to changing world market prices and as there is a limit to natural resources, long-term planning is impossible. Multinational companies have exploited the situation and have set up factories in developing countries to take advantage of cheap labour, relaxed pollution laws and new marketing opportunities.

Several attempts have been made to close the development gap. The approaches centre on aid packages and investment programmes. However, countries can become dependent on aid programmes which can add to their problems. Investment programmes have helped the economies of LEDCs by developing their manufacturing industries. Investment programmes will only work in a stable environment and the political tensions in some developing countries, which can result in war, do not help economic development.

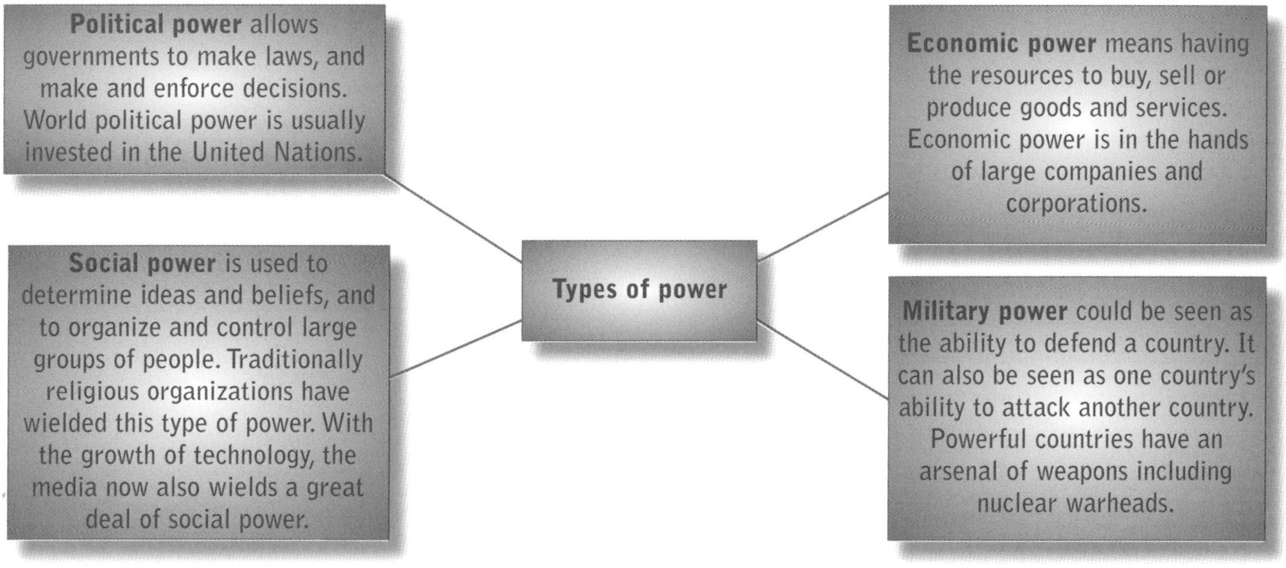

Political power allows governments to make laws, and make and enforce decisions. World political power is usually invested in the United Nations.

Social power is used to determine ideas and beliefs, and to organize and control large groups of people. Traditionally religious organizations have wielded this type of power. With the growth of technology, the media now also wields a great deal of social power.

Types of power

Economic power means having the resources to buy, sell or produce goods and services. Economic power is in the hands of large companies and corporations.

Military power could be seen as the ability to defend a country. It can also be seen as one country's ability to attack another country. Powerful countries have an arsenal of weapons including nuclear warheads.

Figure 8.2 Types of power

Fairtrade, improving working conditions

Trading practices

The World Trade Organization

Trade is the movement of goods and services between different areas or countries. Most countries rely on trade as a major source of income. Trade agreements regulate the import and export of goods between countries. The World Trade Organization, which is a UN agency, meets to discuss issues relating to trade and the operation of agreements. It can intervene in disputes. Countries or individual companies may refer issues to the World Trade Organization if they feel that they are being unfairly treated. Many people believe that the free trade agreements in force are unfair on LEDCs and that fair trade agreements are needed which value the input of workers.

Free trade versus Fairtrade

Many countries belong to free trade associations or other trading groups. The main aim of these trading groups is to encourage trade between particular countries and to protect the industries and interests of the member countries. One of the largest trading groups is the EU.

Free trade uses the raw materials of the LEDCs which have to export them at low prices. This has led to the rise of multinational manufacturers who move into developing countries at the expense of small local businesses and co-operatives. To keep prices down environmental issues have often been neglected and damage has ensued.

Fairtrade agreements aim to give people in LEDCs the chance to benefit from trade and investment rather than suffering from exploitation. Fairtrade organizations want to stop abuse and improve the working conditions of people by improving economic and social development. Fairtrade organizations aim to reduce overheads, increase the amount of profit given to the workers, encourage re-investment, and shift processing and packaging to LEDCs to boost incomes.

The impact of multinational companies

Giant multinational companies are increasingly influential in the world's economy. These multinational companies are operated by a small number of people. They have developed steadily over many years within the market economy and are firm upholders of the capitalist ideal of free trade. The largest can match, or exceed, the size and scale of some nations in wealth, power and trading. For example, in 1997 the GDP (gross domestic product is the total value of goods produced by a country or company in a year) of General Motors was $164 billion and the GDP of Wal-Mart stores $105 billion. The GDP of Norway was $153 billion and the GDP of Israel $98 billion.

Multinational companies have grown in two ways:

- By natural growth – through the creation of products that sell well. The profits from these products are re-invested in the company to enable it to research, develop and produce new consumer goods.
- By merger and acquisition – through mergers with other companies producing similar services and products. Examples of mergers are the joining of Glaxo and SmithKline drug companies in 2000 and of the Lloyds and TSB banks in 1999.

As a result of mergers and acquisitions, multinational companies have moved their operations to various countries in the world, including LEDCs, where conditions for maximizing production and profit were available. Multinational companies look for a location with appropriate transport networks, cheaper labour and suitable incentives from the government of the country, for example low rents or grants. The changes in the location of production have affected the employment patterns in countries at different stages of development.

Multinational are the new global culture

The development of communication technology has been a further factor in the growth of multinationals. Global communication is now easy and speedy and a decision made at corporate level in New York can be in operation in India in minutes.

One example of multinational companies influencing change and promoting internal development in LEDCs (which has rapidly changed them into newly industrialized countries (NICs)) can be seen in Taiwan. Multinational companies encouraged and were a role model for internal development. Now Taiwan has twelve multinational companies each with a market value of over $2.5 billion. These companies have expanded into other areas of east Asia where cheaper labour for manufacturing can be found.

Activities

1. Should the world have a free or a fair trade system? Discuss.
2. Should multinational companies be expected to stop exploitation in developing countries? Discuss.

Aid

Aid is the transfer of money, goods and expertise from one country (the donor) to another (the recipient). Aid is usually given freely, but sometimes low rates of interest are charged on loans or conditions are attached to the goods and services provided. Aid falls into three categories.

Bilateral aid

Bilateral aid is usually given by one country to another in the form of a low interest loan for a specific project. It may require the recipient to enter a trade agreement with the donor. Such agreements are often linked to an order of defence weapons by the recipient. Bilateral aid is given by the UK and France to their former colonies. Multilateral aid is the money given by governments to international agencies. The agencies decide how the money will be spent. Many of these agencies work under the UN. Although these agencies relay the money to areas for development, they are often slow to act because of the bureaucracy surrounding them.

Voluntary aid

Voluntary aid is given by non-government organizations (NGOs). These organizations are mainly charities such as Oxfam, Christian Aid and Save the Children. Most of the charities are based in industrialized countries and they raise money through public appeals, regular voluntary donations, mail order and charity shops. Their aid is more closely targeted to local needs and is usually very effective.

Relief aid is a short-term measure which deals with emergency situations. It is usually given in response to a natural disaster such as a flood, drought or earthquake. Food, medical help, water purification equipment, clothing and blankets are supplied to give relief to survivors.

Development aid

Development aid is given as a long-term solution. It aims to increase a country's level of development by improving the quality of life of its people. Measures include improving health care, providing practical help for farmers, and developing local co-operatives and community projects and initiatives. More and more aid agencies would like to concentrate on development aid as it emphasizes sustainable long-term developments which are community based and promote self-sufficiency.

Development aid is all about self-help, not charity

UN aid agencies

Aid is a major aspect of the work of the UN. It gives relief aid to countries from its funds and usually co-ordinates the funding given by individual countries to cope with emergency situations.

Developmental aid, which is intended for longer-term projects such as immunization and providing clean water, is usually supported by NGOs, for example Oxfam or Christian Aid. The following are examples of UN aid agencies:

- The World Health Organization (WHO) aims to improve the health of the world's people. When it was first established in 1948, the organization concentrated on basic physical health. It tried to eliminate some of the many diseases which attacked the developing world. In recent times, the WHO has tried to promote healthy living. This includes nutritional advice and mental health support. It also deals with the UN's response to world disease such as AIDS.
- The UN Development Programme (UNDP) aims to support countries as they strive to achieve sustainable development. The UNDP is usually involved in activities in developing countries. A country may choose to improve its systems of education, transport, communications or healthcare. The funding for such special projects would come from the UNDP.
- The World Food Programme provides food aid. Based in Rome, its aim is to eliminate world hunger. The programme deals with emergency relief, aid in times of natural disaster and long-term development schemes.
- The UN Fund for Population Activities was established to help countries with population growth strategies. It gives support with education and training as well as family planning development. Unlike other UN funds, this fund is upheld from voluntary contributions from member states.

Activity

Put together information to provide a case study of an aid organization.

The World Food Programme distributing food

Sustainable development

What is sustainable development?

Sustainable development could be defined as 'development which meets the needs of the present without compromising the ability of future generations to meet their own needs' (Bruntland Commission 1987). It means that we should treat the world in such a way that we ensure a better quality of life for everyone, now and for generations to come.

The 1992 Rio Summit

In 1992 the first United Nations Earth Summit was held in Rio de Janeiro, Brazil. This summit promised renewed effort to tackle the main threats to our existence – poverty, hunger, war and environmental destruction. Probably the most significant of the agreements to emerge from this summit was Agenda 21, an action plan for moving towards sustainable development in the twenty-first century. More than 178 governments adopted the agenda and, as a result, the Commission on Sustainable Development (CSD) was created to monitor and report on progress made on the agreements signed in Rio.

Agenda 21 is based on the slogan, 'Think globally, act locally' and is a blueprint on how to make development socially, economically and environmentally sustainable. Governments, regions, local councils, businesses, industry, local communities and individuals are expected to play their part and contribute to the objectives of Local Agenda 21.

Outcomes of the Rio Summit

Though the conference in Rio de Janeiro generated much enthusiasm and commitment to action, many people thought that the Earth Summit was over-ambitious in its aim to address issues such as biodiversity. In the UK, local councils have been required to adopt

Agriculture
Atmosphere
Biodiversity
Biotechnology
Capacity-building
Consumption and production patterns
Demographics
Desertification and drought
Education and awareness
Energy
Finance
Forests
Freshwater
Health
Human settlements
Indicators
Industry
Information
Integrated decisions
International law
Institutional matters
Land management
Major groups
Mountains
Oceans and seas
Poverty
Science
Small islands
Sustainable tourism
Technology
Toxic chemicals
Trade and environment
Transport
Waste (hazardous)
Waste (radioactive)
Waste (solid)

Figure 8.3 Agenda 21 issues

resident George Bush, USA – key opponent of the Kyoto Protocol

Agenda 21 policies for sustainable development. Despite this activity in the UK, many people believe that there is little sign of improvement and that little has been achieved.

One of the main stumbling blocks to the success of the Rio Summit was the response of the USA. The USA refused to sign the Biodiversity Treaty, fearing for its biotechnology industry. It complained about the transfer of control for biotechnology to the LEDCs from where the raw materials for research come as it wanted the freedom to research into genetic 'pools', many of which exist in LEDCs. As a result many people complained that the USA hindered the negotiations at Rio. The USA believes that measures to protect the environment might interfere with the workings of the free market or reduce the rate of economic growth. Many people believe that no treaty or solution will work without US support.

The Kyoto Protocol

The third conference on climatic change took place in December 1997 in Kyoto, Japan. Over 160 countries took part including all European nations. The conference adopted the Kyoto Protocol which agreed the following:

- MEDCs to reduce greenhouse emissions by 5 per cent below 1990 levels by 2012
- LEDCs to continue to reduce carbon levels to 1990 levels by 2005.

MEDCs could reach these targets by

- increasing energy conservation measures in industry, housing and transport sectors
- introducing stricter standards in cars and electrical appliances
- encouraging sustainability by increasing environment-related activities such as recycling.

The USA has not accepted the Kyoto Protocol.

A local recycling area

Local authority responses

To meet the objectives of Local Agenda 21, local authorities around the globe were requested to:

- enter into a dialogue with citizens, local organizations and private enterprises
- adopt a local Agenda 21
- through consultation reach a consensus with all groups in the local community
- acquire information needed for formulating the best strategies for development
- increase household awareness of sustainable development issues
- assess and modify existing programmes, policies, laws and regulations in line with Agenda 21 objectives.

At a local level, councils would be required to make plans to address such issues as:

- conserving energy and managing air quality to prevent fuel poverty and climate change
- buying environmentally friendly goods and services and managing waste to reduce present levels of consumption
- maintaining the variety of plants and animals in the local area and protecting the access of residents to the countryside
- encouraging people to travel on foot, by bicycle or on public transport to reduce car congestion and air pollution
- considering the environment in all land use planning decisions to ensure sustainable development.

Every local authority in the UK was required to consult with local people and to create an action plan which set local priorities and objectives as well as targets to achieve these priorities.

Achieving sustainable development

To achieve sustainable development will require individuals, communities and businesses to accept the challenge and change their way of life. We are using the world's resources at a greater rate than they can be replaced and, although the world is large, sooner or later the resources will run out. We must learn not to pollute the air, water and soil. We must create less waste and stop harming the environment. Much of this change can take place at an individual level, but large industries and organizations must change their policies and play their part too.

People across the UK in local organizations and schools are making a difference to their environment by getting involved with schemes and projects in their local community. Schemes are arranged by groups such as the environmental charity Groundwork, the UK's biggest environmental regeneration charity, and Community Service Volunteers, who organize national Make a Difference Day (MADD).

Activities

1 Contact your local council and ask for its Agenda 21 information. Make notes on the strategic objectives for your area.

2 Make a list of five things you could do to be more environmentally friendly. Discuss this with a partner.

3 Do you think that sustainable development is achievable? Discuss in groups.

Case study: Greenpeace – international agents of change

About Greenpeace

Greenpeace is an international organization with 2.5 million supporters in 158 countries. As an independent organization it relies on individual membership and support to fund its campaigns for effective environmental solutions. Greenpeace was founded in 1971 when a group of like-minded individuals set out in a boat to protest about nuclear weapons testing off Canada. Today, Greenpeace has five ships it can mobilize to go anywhere in the world.

Greenpeace is still committed to non-violent direct action to bring about change. It communicates with over 6000 businesses and governments to persuade them that reforms are necessary to ensure a more efficient and cleaner environment. Greenpeace is concerned with a wide range of environmental and biodiverse causes and is currently active in 35 countries across the world. Perhaps Greenpeace is best known for its campaign to stop commercial whaling.

Non-violent direct action

Non-violent direct action is designed to:

- raise people's awareness of an issue
- put pressure on people in authority to change things
- object to injustices in society
- ultimately change the situation.

The Indian pacifist leader Mahatma Ghandi said, 'In non-violence the masses have a weapon which enables a child, a woman, or even a decrepit old man to resist the mightiest government successfully'. The US black civil rights leader Martin Luther King believed that the only way to achieve equality and change society's views was by non-violent and peaceful forms of protest. He explained the Non-Violent Creed as:

To resist without bitterness
To be cursed and not reply
To be beaten and not hit back.

The first Greenpeace ship – The Phyllis Cormack

Greenpeace with the whales

Greenpeace launched its anti-whaling campaign in 1975, when
populations of the great whales had plummeted to crisis levels.
Most whales had been depleted by a whaling industry that
knew no bounds. Some species were on the brink of extinction.

Using high-profile, non-violent direct actions at sea, public outreach and political lobbying, Greenpeace was instrumental in securing a moratorium on commercial whaling from the International Whaling Commission (IWC). This took effect in 1986, coupled with an international trade ban on whale products by the Convention on the International Trade in Endangered Species (CITES).

Nine countries were whaling when the moratorium took effect and seven ended their activities by 1990. Japan and Norway continued to hunt whales commercially. Today, these countries are pushing to lift the ban on whaling, which will have a devastating impact on the world's remaining whales.

The Greenpeace campaign is part of an international effort to communicate a simple but urgent message:

The time has come to protect whales permanently and end commercial whaling forever.

We are leading the global struggle through:

1 taking non-violent direct action against whalers
2 bearing witness to whaling and communicating the truth back to the world
3 working with the regional whale watching industry to promote it as a viable alternative to whaling
4 public education in countries around the world, including Japan and Norway
5 political lobbying in countries that have influence at the IWC and the CITES
6 participation in annual meetings of the IWC and CITES.

Greenpeace intends to continue this effort until the world's whale populations are protected, permanently, from commercial whaling.

Figure 8.4 Adapted from the Greenpeace website. To visit their website go to www.heinemann.co.uk/hotlinks and insert express code 8109P.

Figure 8.5 Adapted from the Greenpeace membership leaflet

Five recent Greenpeace successes

1999 After ten years of campaigning, food manufacturers and UK supermarkets remove genetically modified ingredients from their products.

1999 Greenpeace launches its campaign to halt illegal logging in the Amazon rainforest. Greenpeace have already been instrumental in stopping all new mahogany logging concessions there.

2000 The British government finally rejects climate damaging refrigerants – hydrofluorocarbons (HFCs) – and acknowledges the advantages of greenfreeze technology pioneered by Greenpeace.

2001 As part of the global campaign for sustainable waste management, Greenpeace action closes the Sheffield incinerator and prevents it emitting harmful toxic gases and ash. This incinerator was demolished.

2001 Greenpeace and Power launch 'Juice' – a clean electricity product at no extra cost. It will supply 50 000 homes and promote the development of a specific windfarm out at sea.

Tokyo stirs frenzy for whalemeat

From Robert Whymant in Tokyo

JAPAN is using ice-cream and musicals to win hearts and stomachs in its battle to lift the ban on commercial whaling at a critical International Whaling Commission (IWC) meeting in May.

Loudspeaker vans are touring the nation urging people to eat whalemeat and back the abolition of a 16-year-old moratorium on whale hunting. . ..

Motoji Nagasawa, who heads Greenpeace Japan's anti-whaling campaign, said: 'The government's strategy is to . . . make it appear whalemeat is important to the Japanese diet – the reverse of the truth.'

As in previous years, Japan plans to seek the resumption of coastal whaling when the IWC meets in Shimonoseki, western Japan . . .. The clash with anti-whaling countries such as the United States and Britain is expected to be particularly fierce this year, because Japan says that it intends to step up 'scientific' killing of whales, including an endangered species.

In 1986 Tokyo complied reluctantly with the ban on commercial whaling, but quickly began bringing in carcasses disguised as 'scientific research whaling'. Last year Japanese whalers brought home 440 from Antarctica, and 158 from the northwest Pacific, for sale to restaurants after perfunctory tests to determine diet and migration patterns.

Millions of pounds are being spent to mask an embarrassing fact: that a majority of Japanese would prefer whale-watching to whale-eating.

'It's a complete deception. Nobody in today's Japan considers whalemeat important to our diet,' Mr Nagasawa said. 'There's none in my supermarket. And there's no vital economic interest. Only about 300 people work full-time in whaling.'

A recent government survey said that about 70 per cent of Japanese back a resumption of whaling, and nearly 90 per cent had eaten whalemeat at least once. The findings were at odds with a survey conducted by MORI with a Japanese partner two years ago on behalf of Greenpeace.

Figure 8.6 Adapted from the *Times*, 23 March 2002

Activities

1. Japan continues to whale for 'scientific' reasons. Japan caught 598 whales in 2001. Should this be allowed? Discuss in groups.
2. Use the Greenpeace website to list five current Greenpeace campaigns.
3. Whaling and eating whale meat has been a part of culture in countries like Japan for many years. Should any country or group of countries impose cultural values on another? Discuss in groups.
4. Whales are harpooned. Is this method of killing acceptable? Discuss in pairs.

Check it out

What you should have learned from this chapter

Look at the areas of study in the table. You should now know and understand the terminology and concepts that we have explored in Chapter 8: World trade and overseas aid.

The activities and questions in the chapter, and the worksheets your teacher will have worked through with you, should have helped you to learn about this topic.

If some of the areas are not clear, read through the pages again. If you are still not sure ask your teacher to explain them again.

Area of study	Page
The development gap	121
The Third World	122
The World Trade Organization	124
Free trade and Fairtrade	124
Multinational companies	125
Aid programmes	126
Agenda 21 and sustainable development	128
Local responses to Agenda 21	130

You should be able to answer all the following questions. These are short answer questions similar to those that will appear in Section A of the written exam paper that you will sit at the end of the course.

The knowledge and concepts covered in this chapter will also be tested in longer, more detailed questions in Section B and D of the exam paper.

?

1. What is meant by the 'development gap'?
2. What is the Third World?
3. What do the initials MEDC and LEDC stand for? What do the terms mean?
4. What is a Fairtrade agreement?
5. List three types of aid.
6. Name three charities which work to provide voluntary aid.
7. What is Agenda 21?
8. How has your community responded to Agenda 21?

An LEDC favela, São Paulo, Brazil

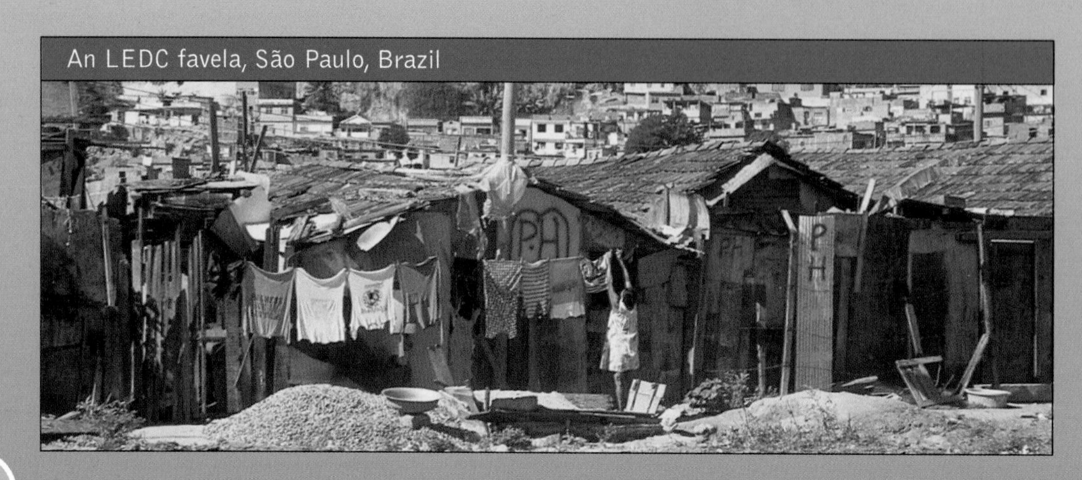

9 Exploring global issues – the human and environmental problems

Every issue raised and explored in the following pages provides you with a starting point for discussion and debate in the classroom and beyond. You are given the opportunity to formulate and express your opinions on a range of human and environmental global issues. You should always research discussion topics carefully so you can present your views and arguments in an informed and structured way. Remember that most of the issues you will study promote strong feelings in many people. Try to be honest and express yourself clearly while being polite and non-offensive. Try to empathize with the other person and be accepting of views that contradict your own.

Debating global issues

Figure 9.1 From 'A curriculum for global citizenship, Oxfam'

The key elements of responsible global citizenship

Knowledge and understanding

- Social justice and equality
- Diversity
- Globalization and interdependence
- Sustainable development
- Peace and conflict

Skills

- Critical thinking
- Ability to argue effectively
- Ability to challenge injustice and inequalities
- Respect for people and things
- Co-operation and conflict resolution

Values and attitudes

- Sense of identity and self-esteem
- Empathy
- Commitment to social justice and equality
- Value and respect for diversity
- Concern for the environment and commitment to sustainable development
- Belief that people can make a difference

As you work through the issues outlined, you should question the basis of the arguments presented and decide whether you agree. Keep a record of the questions you would like answering. The writer has made every effort to be factual and free from bias, but there may be issues in which you could question the writer's motives. You should feel free to do so! As a citizen, you have the right to understand fully the systems of which you are a part as a producer, as a consumer, as one of the world's people. Start to ask yourself and other people questions about the processes and the outcomes which affect the world's population and the planet's resources. Below are some examples of questions which you could investigate.

Am I tolerant of other nations and cultures?

Is poverty inevitable?

To make fundamental changes and to develop sustainable lifestyles, what needs to happen at local, national and international level?

Are current world trade practices ethical? Who gains? Who loses?

Poverty

A basic human right

Everyone has the right to 'a standard of living adequate for health and well-being of themselves and their family, including food, clothing, housing and medical care'. This is the statement made in Article 25 of the UN Universal Declaration of Human Rights. Living in poverty means that people do not have the means to provide these basic needs for themselves and their families. Despite many improvements in the world's overall poverty figures, there is still a great deal of human deprivation and degradation, especially in developing countries. A 1997 UN Report stated that the poverty in the world had been reduced. In the southern hemisphere infant mortality rates had been cut by almost 60 per cent and more than 75 per cent of the population can now expect to live beyond the age of 40. The everyday reality is that poverty is a major cause of disease and illness, poor educational opportunity, unnecessary migration and despair, which often leads to conflict.

How is poverty measured?

The wealth of a country is determined by how many goods it produces. The most widely used indicator of a country's development and status is GNP (Gross National Product) per head of population. The GNP is calculated by adding up the values of all the goods and services produced by the country during the year. The total amount is divided by the population to give the GNP per head. The result is given in US dollars to make the comparison between countries easier.

GNP is known as an economic indicator. GNP is a more reliable indicator for MEDCs than it is for LEDCs. As MEDCs have more information about population and trade figures available to them, they can work out the statistics of GNP to a more reliable level than LEDCs. Also, in developing countries many people live in subsistence farming communities so they do not produce items to be sold and their efforts are not included in the calculation of GNP.

Other measures of development could be used, while accepting that reliable statistics for comparing countries are difficult to obtain. Alternatives to economic indicators are social indicators which measure improvements in health or housing, or The Physical Quality of Life Index which is an overall value based on

Children living in urban poverty

combining the values of three measures – life expectancy, infant mortality and literacy. Alternative measures of development could include economic and social factors combined.

A global view of poverty

The majority of the world's richest countries are in the northern hemisphere (except for Australia and New Zealand). About 20 per cent of the world's population live in the developed countries, yet this 20 per cent controls about 80 per cent of the world's wealth. This means that there is an unequal distribution of wealth throughout the world.

In all countries poverty is relative and there is an economic spectrum from very rich to very poor. However, very few people in the developed world live in real or absolute poverty, which means that a person earns and owns almost nothing and that every day is a struggle for survival.

Finance

The World Bank and the IMF

When a bank lends money it makes a loan. It will charge interest on this loan by agreeing an interest rate with the borrower. The borrower is now in debt. That means the borrower owes the bank the sum of money it borrowed as well as the interest which it will pay annually for the length of the loan. To help a country develop its education system, a bank might agree to lend it £10 million to be paid back over twenty years at an interest rate of 10 per cent. In simple terms, this means that the country will need to pay £1 million interest per year. If the country fails to make the repayments of the loan at the correct time, the amount owed will increase at the rate of interest (10 per cent). The longer it takes to pay, the more the country will need to pay back and the longer it will be in debt.

To borrow money from the World Bank, a country needs to be a member of the International Monetary Fund (IMF). The World Bank is the main international organization that lends money to finance projects in developing countries. The IMF is responsible for managing the world economy by creating stability in trade between countries. To achieve this objective the IMF places conditions or restrictions on the money loaned. The IMF has based its operation on the system of free trade which benefits the powerful Western nations. Some people believe that the time has come to change to a system of fair trade which will benefit the developing nations.

Third World debt

In the1970s when large profits were made in the oil industry, the proceeds were deposited in Western banks. The banks had plenty of money so they loaned it to Africa, Latin America and Asia. Many countries have found it difficult to repay the loans. This could be due to inflation, natural disaster, political unrest, fluctuations in world trade or war. As a result some African countries are falling deeper and deeper into debt. Indeed some African countries spend more on debt repayments than they are currently spending on education and health combined. Debt repayments do not leave finance for industrial development or building the country's infrastructure. Many people believe that the Western world should do more to write off the debts even though this would reduce the income of the donor country.

Demonstrating to abolish Third World debt

Human rights abuses

The background

The United Nations Universal Declaration of Human Rights was signed in 1948. It was designed as a safeguard against injustice and cruelty and its aim was to protect the human rights of people around the world. In its first section it states that 'All human beings are born free and equal in dignity and rights. They are endowed with reason and conscience, and should act towards one another in a spirit of brotherhood'. The United Nations believes that every human being has rights which are covered by law and morality. The rights in the declaration cover a wide variety of issues including freedom from slavery, the right to peaceful assembly and freedom of movement.

The UN Commission on Human Rights was set up to monitor the declaration's operation. It monitors countries for human rights abuses relating to imprisonment, torture, the death penalty, and sexual and racial discrimination. If the commission has evidence of human rights abuses, it will refer the matter to the United Nations Council which will decide whether to take action against the offending country. Political pressure to deal with human rights abuses may involve economic sanctions, observers in the country or, rarely, military action.

Non-government organizations

The United Nations Commission and other UN bodies are helped in their endeavours by the work of NGOs like Amnesty International and ACT (Action by Christians against Torture). In some parts of the world people are having their freedoms and even their lives taken away simply because they think differently from their government and speak against their policies. In some cases the person has spoken in private to a friend about political concerns and has not made any public statement.

Amnesty International, founded in 1961, investigates and tries to stop such human rights violations. Amnesty International has over 1 million members in 150 countries and is the world's largest voluntary body working to protect human rights. It aims to:

- seek the release of all prisoners of conscience
- obtain a fair and prompt trial for all political prisoners detained without charge or trial
- abolish torture and the death penalty.

This child works in a carpet factory in Varanasi, India

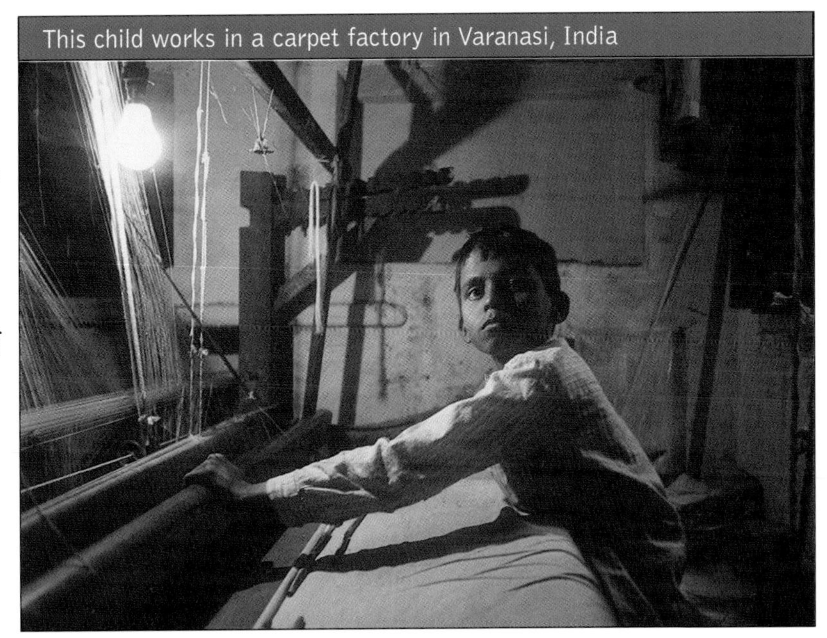

What are human rights abuses?

There are many examples in the world today of the violation of human rights. Perhaps the most obvious violation is that more than 1 billion people are living in extreme poverty. Human rights are abused in many areas of life, for example when people:

- are not allowed freedom of expression
- are not allowed the freedom to practise a religion of their choice either in public or in private
- are tortured
- are not granted the right to a fair trial
- are discriminated against on the grounds of race, disability, sex or religion
- are denied a basic standard of living
- are not allowed asylum from persecution in a different country.

Some groups would argue that denying people the right to die (euthanasia) contravenes a human right. Euthanasia is not allowed under British law. Others would say that abortion abuses the rights of the unborn child. Abortion is legal in Britain.

The rights of the child

Children are the most vulnerable group in any society. Where there are no parents or supportive adults to protect their rights, they are often abused and exploited. In 1989 the UN produced the Declaration of the Rights of the Child. This sets out the rights of the child with respect to:

- survival – children should have a decent standard of living and good health
- development – children have the right to a full and free education
- protection – children have the right to be protected from slavery, exploitation, cruelty or enforced separation from their family
- participation – children have the right to express an opinion on any issue that effects them including their health and education.

There is still much to be done to meet the aims of this declaration. For example, in some countries children work long hours and are poorly paid. It is estimated that 17.5 million children under the age of fourteen work for small rewards in India.

The issue of arms and weapons

The background

The world spends more on arms than on anything else. Although the amount of money spent on arms has fallen, it still accounts for approximately 3 per cent of the world's gross domestic product. Developing countries buy over half the world's arms and spend 66 per cent more on military strength than on education. MEDCs are the main exporters of arms, in particular the USA, France and Britain. The countries which buy the most arms are India, Iraq, Japan and Saudi Arabia.

Biological and chemical weapons can kill large numbers of people. Biological weapons include the use of viruses and bacteria which cause death in humans. Chemical weapons include toxic substances which will kill or disable people or poison food or water supplies.

The arms trade

The arms trade describes the manufacture and sale of a wide range of military weapons, vehicles and equipment. It refers to items such as fighter aircraft, tanks, missiles, guns and grenades. The British Government is one agency that sells arms through the Defence Export Services Organization (DESO). The DESO will organize an arms exhibition, will invite other countries to attend and encourage them to buy the arms. The government might offer aid to a developing country to enable it to build roads in return for an arms deal or it may offer export credits. If the country who has bought the arms finds it difficult to pay the agreed amount, it is not uncommon for the debt to be written off.

One result of the arms trade can be an arms race. This happens when one country buys military equipment and neighbouring countries feel threatened so buy arms themselves. Countries then compete against each other to ensure that they have adequate military strength.

Nuclear weapons

Nuclear weapons were first developed by the USA during World War II (1939–45). Only two nuclear bombs have ever been dropped in populated areas. This happened in 1945 when the USA dropped bombs on the cities of Hiroshima and Nagasaki in Japan.

There has been a marked increase in the number of countries possessing nuclear missiles. In 1999, India and Pakistan tested nuclear warheads and declared that they had nuclear technology at their disposal. One reason for the increase is that improved technology has made it cheaper for countries to develop nuclear missiles. Another reason is that nuclear information is easily accessed from the Internet. Supporters of nuclear weapons argue that they are necessary to protect the country and prevent war. Critics say that the massive expense of nuclear weapons (one missile costs $12 million) could be spent on the environment and overseas aid.

Hiroshima, after dropping the nuclear bomb, 1945

Landmines

A landmine is an explosive device which is buried under, on, or near the ground. It is designed to cause an explosion when a weight, usually in the form of a person or a vehicle, passes near to it or over it. There are many places in the world where landmines, which were used in times of conflict, have been left in the ground. These landmines continue to cause injury and death to the local residents. Over 10 000 people are killed each year by landmines while 16 000 are injured or maimed. In addition to injury, landmines restrict the access of local people to amenities such as water, fields and shelter. Removing landmines is expensive and time consuming. For every 5000 landmines removed, one skilled person will be killed and two people will be injured.

Although international law makes it clear that in times of war and conflict civilians should be protected as far as possible and never directly attacked, landmines are still used widely. The 1999 Ottawa Treaty banned the use of landmines. By 2000, 89 countries had signed the treaty. However, one developed country, the USA, refused to sign the treaty.

Landmine victim

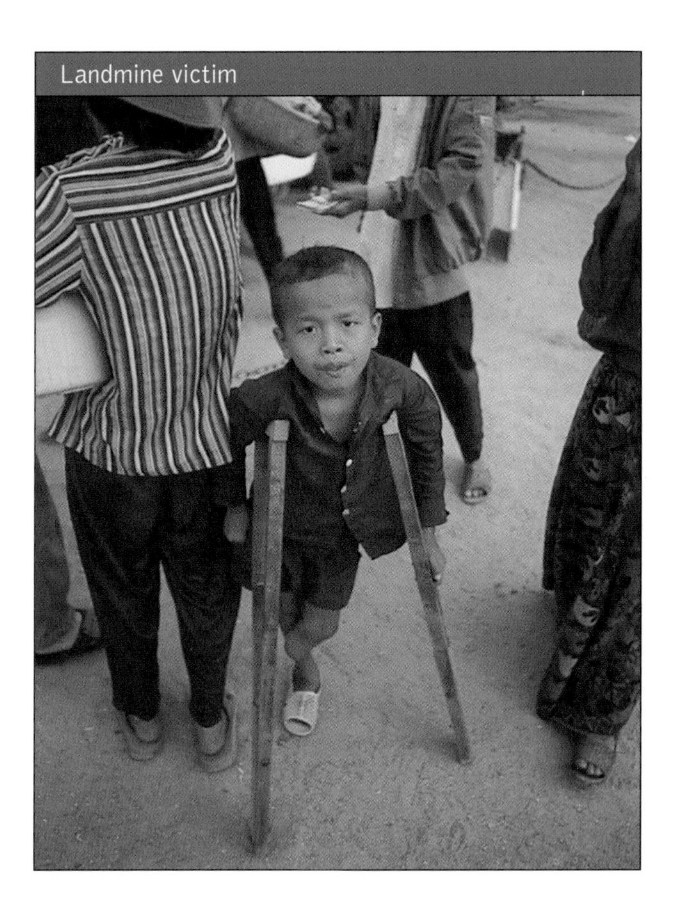

Global warming

The background

Global warming is not a new phenomenon. The world has seen many changes in temperature during its 4600 million year history. These changes have taken place naturally over a period of time. What is worrying scientists today is the speed at which change is taking place and the human factors that are promoting this rapid rate of change. As a result of climatic change, droughts, floods and hurricanes have affected places that are not used to such extreme weather conditions. Global warming is causing ice sheets to melt and the sea levels to rise. This will cause flooding in low-lying coastal areas.

How does it happen?

If there is too much carbon in the atmosphere, more heat from the Earth's surface is trapped. This is known as the greenhouse effect. Greenhouse gases, such as methane, water vapour, chlorofluorocarbons (CFCs) and nitrogen oxides, trap the heat from the sun in the atmosphere and the result is global warming. An increase in any of these gases will cause the global temperature to rise and can cause a hole to form in the Earth's protective ozone layer which exposes the Earth to more ultraviolet rays from the sun. These holes in the ozone layer also expose the Earth to increased heat.

Some factors affecting global warming

- Solar heat in the form of radiation passes through the atmosphere and warms the land and sea.
- Carbon dioxide (CO_2) traps the heat reflected back from the Earth. As more CO_2 is produced, more heat is trapped.
- CFCs from aerosols and refrigeration plants trap heat in the upper atmosphere and thin the ozone layer.
- CO_2 comes from burning forests and rotting trees.
- Waste from both people and animals produces the greenhouse gas methane.
- Burning coal, gas and oil adds carbon to the atmosphere. This carbon traps heat.
- The number of vehicles in the world is growing. Oil and petrol emissions cause greenhouse gases.
- The use of fertilizers which are nitrogen based adds more nitrous oxide, a greenhouse gas, to the atmosphere.
- The oceans and seas absorb CO_2 from the atmosphere, but now more CO_2 is produced than the oceans can absorb.

What needs to be done?

Environmentalists argue that we need to reduce the amount of energy we use immediately to reduce the amount of greenhouse gases we produce and so slow down the rate of global warming. This could by done by:

- making our homes and workplaces energy-efficient
- increasing the amount of materials we use that can be recycled
- walking to local shops for our weekly shopping and using public transport instead of private cars for longer journeys.

Friends of the Earth and Greenpeace say that being energy-efficient is not enough and that we need to develop the use of renewable energy sources such as solar panels, hydro-electric generators and wind turbines which do not damage the atmosphere by producing greenhouse gases. Fossil fuels such as coal, oil and gas are being depleted across the world and will soon run out.

A wind farm – a renewable energy source

Acid rain

The background

Rain is always slightly acidic as carbon dioxide is dissolved as the drops of rain fall through the atmosphere. Such acidity is strong enough to dissolve limestone and form interesting rock formations. Tests have shown that the rain in Europe and North America is sometimes one hundred times more acid than the slightly acidic rain which causes erosion. This is because the rain is polluted.

Burning coal, gas and oil and emissions from car exhausts release sulphur dioxide and nitrogen oxides into the atmosphere where they dissolve in the water droplets in the clouds. The pollutants then become part of the water cycle and the result is acid rain.

The prevailing wind can carry the water droplets for great distances before they fall as rain or snow. The south-west prevailing winds mean that some of the pollution produced in the British Isles is blown across the North Sea to Norway and Sweden – countries which produce little pollution of their own.

Scientists have warned that global warming is likely to increase acid rain in the future as higher temperatures can increase the rate of chemical reactions.

The effects of acid rain

In New York State, USA, almost 6 per cent of all the lakes and ponds of the area are badly affected by acid rain. Local people report the loss of fish, birds, otters and other animals from the lakes. This is one example of how acid rain affects the ecosystems of the areas where it is prevalent. Other problems include the destruction of trees particularly in Europe and North America.

Acid rain deposits particles on buildings, statues and bridges and causes corrosion. Buildings made of limestone are particularly at risk. If left untreated, bridges may pose a safety risk, and castles and cathedrals are at risk of crumbling.

Acid rain can have a direct effect on people's health. Dry deposits can cause respiratory problems, coughs and headaches. If water supplies become contaminated then toxic chemicals from the rain can be stored in fruit, vegetables and animals making food a danger to people.

The effects of acid rain in plain view

What can be done?

Acid rain can be reduced but it will require all countries in the world to make and abide by any agreement made and it will be costly to implement. Acid rain can be reduced by:

- decreasing emissions of sulphur dioxide (SO_2) from power stations by burning low sulphur coal or alternative fuels and by introducing technology to remove SO_2 at the end of the process
- decreasing emissions from cars by improving car engines, fitting catalytic converters and using cleaner fuels
- using alternative energy sources such as hydro-electric power and wind, solar and tidal power
- having an international agreement backed by laws and finance in each country
- raising public awareness and changing social habits with respect to saving energy, for example turning off lights, insulating houses, using the car less.

Deforestation

The background

Global wood and paper consumption in 1990 was 1.7 billion cubic metres. It is predicted that this will have increased by 60 per cent by the year 2010. Across the world, forests are being cut down or made into huge plantations to meet the demand for newspapers, writing paper, doors and window frames, laminate flooring, the plethora of junk mail that we face every day and a host of other everyday items based on wood and its pulp. By taking this wood from the world's forests, we threaten the existence of hundreds of plant and animal species and we change the way of life for millions of forest people. In 1650, approximately 60 per cent of the world's land surface was forest. By 2000, this had been reduced to 25 per cent.

The causes of deforestation

The main cause of deforestation is simply the cutting down of trees (see Figure 9.1).

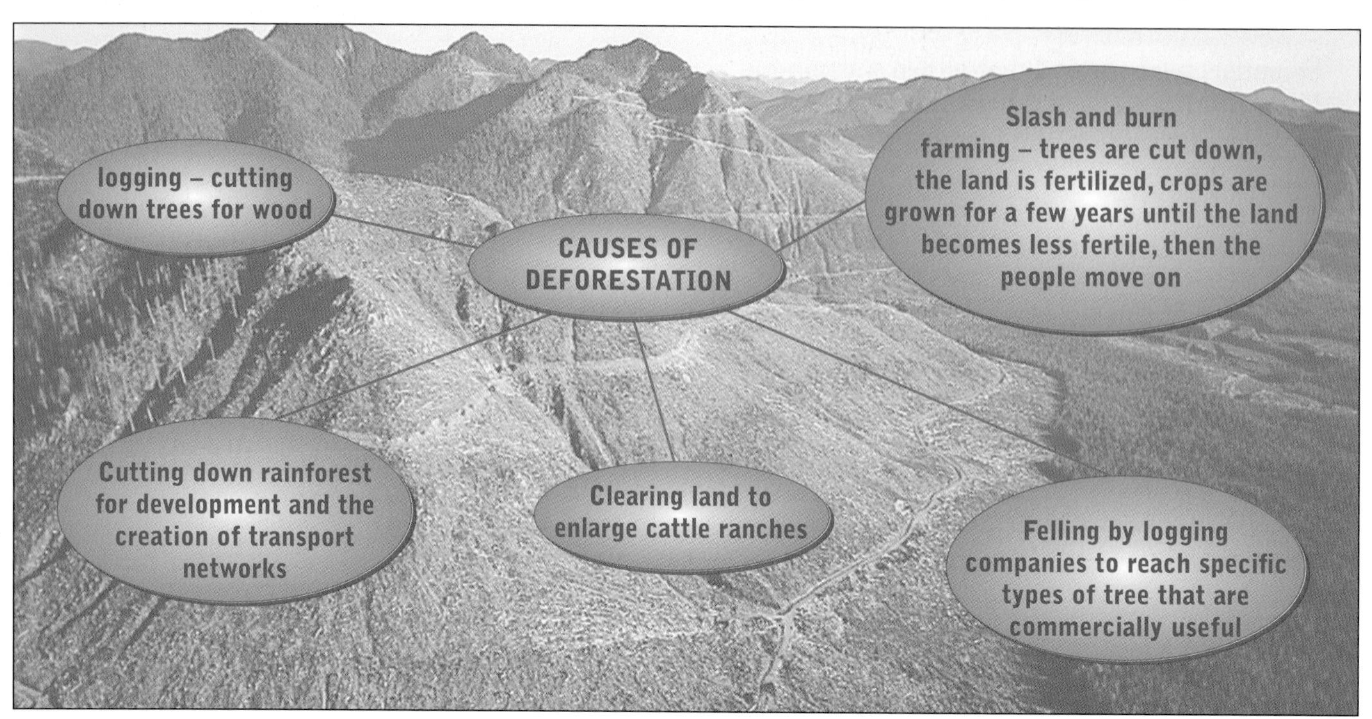

Figure 9.1 The causes of deforestation

Rainforests have faced destruction in Brazil, Colombia, Indonesia, Thailand, Mexico and Nigeria. As these countries are faced by the problems of Third World debt, over-population, war, famine or floods, the governments of these countries argue that they have no alternative. They want their countries to develop and the only way they can make use of their countries' natural resources is through deforestation.

Why save the rainforests?

The rainforests cover only 2 per cent of the world's surface but they are the oldest and the richest of the world's ecosystems. They:

- contain 50 per cent of all the world's living species
- act as 'gene pools' – over 40 per cent of the world's prescribed medicines come from rain forests
- are the home of many indigenous peoples
- anchor the soil in their roots preventing soil erosion
- regulate the balance of gases in the atmosphere reducing the greenhouse effect
- prevent flooding and maintain moisture levels in the atmosphere
- protect soils from sunlight because only 1 per cent of solar radiation can pass through the canopy of the forest.

South American rainforest – a river of destruction

The threat to coniferous forests

Conifers are extremely important for the supply of wood and timber. There are major industries in Scandinavia, Canada and Russia. Sustainable ecological management is practised in most coniferous forests, but the replacement plantations for felled trees are not natural ecosystems and they support fewer species of plants and animals than the natural forests. In June 2000 Greenpeace gave evidence on its website of illegal logging activities in Russia. This is a common problem in Russia and there are currently no punishments.

Sustainable forestry

One way to repair the damage caused by deforestation is sustainable forestry. This is practised by the Forestry Commission in Scotland. It is based on the principle that for every tree that is felled, another is planted in its place. While this practice is approved by environmentalists, they argue that it is necessary to plant additional trees to make up for past deforestation practices.

Protecting the world's ecosystems

What are ecosystems?

In any environment there are rocks and soils, vegetation, living organisms including humans, water, the atmosphere and climate. The relationship between the individual components and their interaction with each other is described as an ecosystem. An ecosystem can be at any scale, from a small pond on a farm to the tropical rainforests or tundra regions.

How do ecosystems work?

The interaction between the component parts of an ecosystem creates a cycle of activity (Figure 9.2). The sunlight is absorbed by plants and passed through the system as food for insects and animals. Other animals consume these insects and animals. The plants, insects and animals act as temporary stores of energy. Each time energy is transferred between organisms it loses some of its power. Eventually the plants and animals die. As they decompose they provide nutrients such as nitrogen and calcium for the soil. These nutrients are then absorbed through the roots of plants and are used to feed the plants. The cycle starts again. Every component of an ecosystem depends upon the others for its survival.

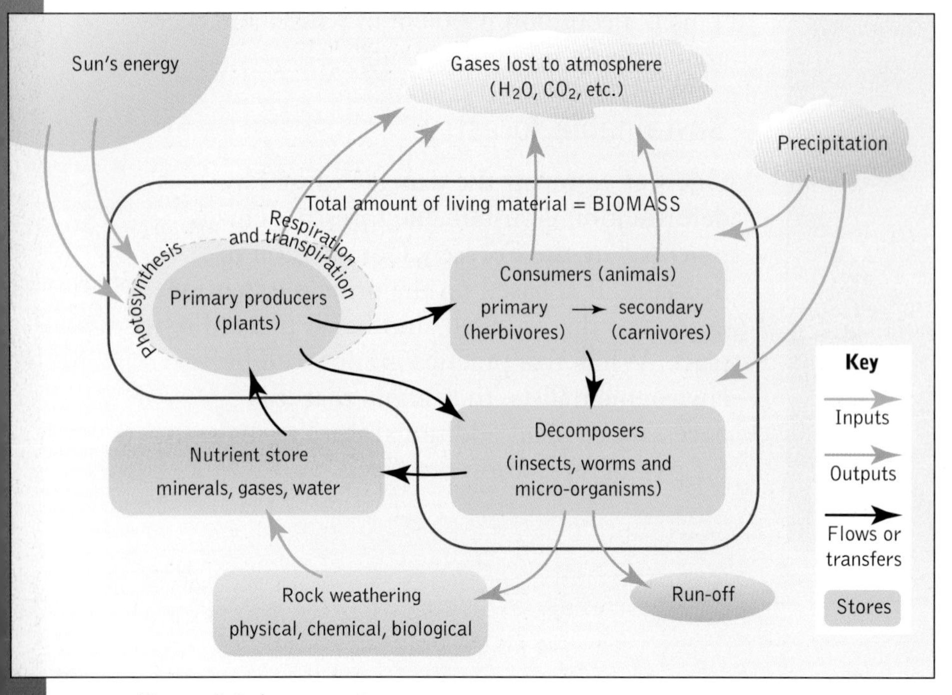

Figure 9.2 An ecosystem

Ecosystems and biodiversity

We rely on our environment to meet our needs. It seems sensible that we should look after our environment for future generations to use as we have used it. This means that we should manage the environment so that a wide variety of wildlife and ecosystems continue to exist. This variety of systems is known as biodiversity. We need to adopt sustainable methods in our use of the environment to ensure that we keep the range of biodiversity in the world and don't cause species extinction.

Managing the world's ecosystems

Ecosystem management is becoming increasingly important. Many ecosystems have been designated as having global scientific significance and have been targeted for conservation. These are known as World Heritage Areas. One World Heritage Area is the Galapagos Islands off the coast of Ecuador. This is an ideal site for conservationists to protect and study. However, the unique wildlife and the exciting volcanic peaks make it a target for tourists. There is obvious conflict between conservation and development efforts. Even though the number of tourists allowed to visit the islands is limited, conservationists still argue that the ecosystem is under threat. Future decisions on the environment should allow for human use while protecting the fragile balance nature has developed.

What are you going to do about it?

We are beginning to realize that our personal habits and actions, social practices and industrial methods affect the balance of the planet and, consequently, the lives of millions of people in other countries. The wealthiest countries in the world are the biggest consumers of energy, minerals and food. Now, we must come to terms with what we have done to the planet. The young people of today are the decision-makers of tomorrow so it will be up to you to change things and increase the Earth's chances of survival. There is much to be done. Every action, no matter how small, will help. This page provides some ideas for you.

It will be up to the youth of today to save the planet for future generations. So don't just sit there – do something!

Join a local group and help in the community.

Write to your MP or local councillor to tell them what you think should be done.

Support some of the organizations mentioned in the book. You could write to tell them you support them or raise money for their efforts.

(Remember that these organizations are charities so if you want a reply enclose a s.a.e.)

Encourage your school, youth club or other group to link with a Third World community.

Join a national or international group and get involved in their activities. (Make sure that your parents have given permission as there is usually a cost to join such organizations.)

Use pump sprays or CFC-free aerosols.

Save water – turn the tap off when you clean your teeth!

Start recycling glass bottles, aluminium cans and paper.

Save electricity – switch off the lights when they are not needed and don't overfill the kettle!

Buy recycled paper products

Re-use your plastic bags.

Walk to school.

Check it out

What you should have learned from this chapter

Look at the areas of study in the table. You should now know and understand the terminology and concepts that we have explored in Chapter 9: Exploring global issues.

The activities and questions in the chapter, and the worksheets your teacher will have worked through with you, should have helped you to learn about this topic.

If some of the areas are not clear, read through the pages again. If you are still not sure then ask your teacher to explain them again.

Area of study	Page
Poverty	136
Finance	137
Human rights abuses	138
The rights of the child	139
Arms and weapons	140
Global warming	141
Acid rain	143
Ecosystems and deforestation	144, 146
Making changes – What will you do?	147

You should be able to answer all the following questions. These are short answer questions similar to those that will appear in Section A of the written exam paper that you will sit at the end of the course.

The knowledge and concepts covered in this chapter will also be tested in longer, more detailed questions in Section B and D of the exam paper.

?

1. How is the wealth of a country measured?
2. Where are most of the world's richest countries?
3. What do IMF stand for?
4. What is the World Bank?
5. Name two NGOs which work to prevent human rights abuse.
6. What is the UN Universal Declaration of Human Rights?
7. When have nuclear weapons been used in war?
8. List three ways we can all help to reduce global warming.
9. Give two effects of acid rain.
10. What is an ecosystem?
11. What is the main cause of deforestation?
12. Name four countries where rainforests are being destroyed.

Coursework and exam techniques

Key ideas

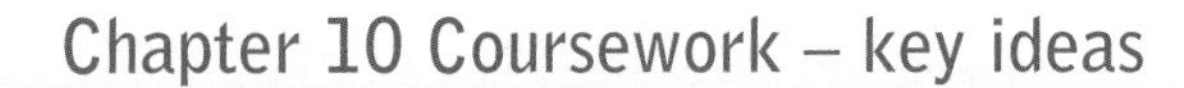

Chapter 10 Coursework – key ideas

* What is coursework?
* What do you need to do?
* Assessment
* Carrying out the coursework

Chapter 11 Exam techniques – key ideas

* The question paper
* A final word

Days of exams are hard – but they can really broaden your horizons . . .

10 Coursework

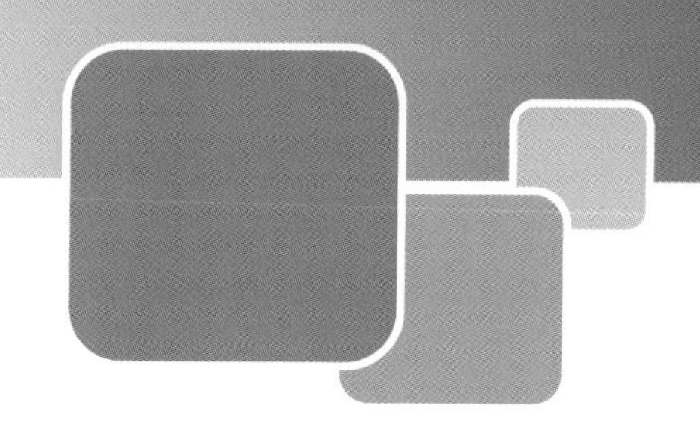

There are two parts to the GCSE exam in Citizenship Studies. One part is the centre-assessed component, usually referred to as coursework, and the other is the final written exam paper taken at the end of the course. Both elements are important. The coursework accounts for 40 per cent of the total marks, and the written paper 60 per cent of the total marks.

What is coursework?

The short course in Citizenship Studies is a brand new GCSE and the coursework is a little different from the coursework that you will be asked to prepare for other subjects.

The purpose of the coursework is for you to take responsibility and participate in a citizenship activity. It may be an activity within your school or in the wider community. No one else can do this for you – it must be your own work. The grade you finally achieve will depend on your own effort and commitment. However, this does not mean that you are completely on your own – your teacher will offer you all the help and guidance possible.

What do you need to do?

You may be given a choice of activities to choose from, or your group may all work around a common task. Your teacher will ensure the activity you are involved in is suitable. You must be able to show that you have planned the activity, taken part in it and written up an account, which also includes other information you have discovered through research. You must then evaluate the activity. All this will be done in stages. Make sure you keep up to date with your work at each stage.

Assessment

The coursework must provide evidence that you have participated in a citizenship activity and that you understand it; and that you have obtained and used information and been able to communicate informed opinions about what you have found. In evaluating the activity you must show the part you have played and the opinions and contributions of other people.

The coursework involves planning, organizing and carrying out an activity which is written up and evaluated. It is then marked by your teacher and may be sent to a moderator, who ensures that standards of marking are the same from all schools. Teachers and moderators work to the same mark scheme, which is divided into four sections:

- planning (10 marks)
- knowledge and understanding of events and roles (10 marks)
- explanation and interpretation of evidence (15 marks)
- evaluation (15 marks).

Another 3 marks can be awarded for how well you communicate your ideas, making a possible total of 53 marks.

Carrying out the coursework

Stage 1 Planning

Once you have determined the activity you are to carry out you must start to plan it.

In your written work you need to give a very clear description of what you are going to do (the aims of the activity) and be able to show why you are doing it (the purpose of the activity) – how it relates to the course, who it will help or who will benefit. The plan you are about to produce is often called an action plan.

Draft out some initial ideas as a brief action plan. Read it again and give the plan a logical structure including all the necessary details. Think about the best way of presenting your action plan. You could use a flow chart for the initial ideas (make sure you include it in your final presentation), then work out a more detailed chart showing:

- the sequence of events
- who will be involved
- when the different events are to take place
- what resources you will need
- if possible, some idea of the timing of events
- what you need to find out, i.e. what research you will need to do.

Your teacher may provide you with a chart to complete, or you may draw one yourself. You may use computers to help you to present your work if you like, but this is not essential.

Good, thoughtful planning is essential for success. Consider very carefully what you are going to do and write the plan in as much detail as you can. Try to think of everything – and if your teacher makes helpful suggestions about things you have omitted, be sure to amend your plan accordingly. Accept the advice given and act on it – you will probably gain extra marks and the activity will run smoothly.

Stage 2 Account of the activity

Now your plan is approved and complete, put the plan into action.

Do your research thoroughly. Consider the presentation of your coursework carefully. If you need to change the action plan because of your findings, that's fine. Write up what you are changing and why – you get marks for being able to make changes and justify them.

While you are involved in the activity you will get to know people quite well in a variety of situations or roles. If the activity is carried out during a short space of time, as soon as it is over it is best to write down your thoughts and reactions to what you did, what others contributed, how they felt, other people's opinions and your own feelings and opinions.

If the activity is going to continue over a period of time it would be sensible to keep a diary of important events or situations that arise including comments on what happened, who was involved, how you felt at the time, or how others were affected.

Now that you have planned, researched and carried out the activity you have to write an account of all that you have done. The marks are awarded in two ways:

- for how you can show your knowledge and understanding of the events that took place and the roles and relationships of all the people who were involved. There is a total of 10 marks for this. Look at your notes or diary that you compiled during the activity and think about what happened, the part you played and the part other people played. In Chapter 1 we looked at the rights and responsibilities of various people. From your knowledge of rights and responsibilities, identify the different roles that you and others have played. What were your responsibilities?
- for explaining and interpreting evidence. There is a total of 15 marks for this. You must show that you understand the purpose of the activity and present all the information you

have found including where the activity took place, the people involved and how the activity fits into the community. Include any regional, national or global links. Analyse the evidence you have collected and present it coherently in a variety of ways. If you can, include a chart, picture, photograph or diagram, to explain the information or data. Form an opinion based on the evidence you have presented. Mention any current issues surrounding the activity – discuss these and show your knowledge.

The write-up

Try to include as many points from the advice above as you can. Gather all the data/information/diary entries/notes that you have for the activity. Think about the order you are going to present it in and the methods of presentation you are going to use. Make sure your report on the activity is concise and informative. Show that you are able to organize and present information clearly and logically, and that you are able to express your opinions.

Start by setting the scene:

- describe the purpose of the activity
- describe where the activity took place
- set the activity in the context of the community and try to relate it to local or regional issues – it is important to show your understanding of this.

Then write about the activity:

- write about your participation in the activity and the people you met
- discuss some of the important concepts you have learned about, such as the rights, roles and responsibilities of all those involved including yourself
- think about questions such as
    - How did you get on with other people?
    - Were they the same age or much older than you?
    - How were you treated?
- Include any written comments from those responsible for the activity or from other pupils you worked with about
    - the activity and your part in it
    - how you worked
    - your attitude towards the activity and other people involved.

To finish the report:

- form your own opinions from the evidence you have presented and state these opinions
- draw conclusions from all that happened during the course of the activity and write them down.

Stage 3: Evaluation

The evaluation is an important section and is worth 15 marks. An evaluation is a critical review of all that went on throughout the activity.

You need to demonstrate:

- why the activity was suitable – you must show that you knew the purpose of what you were involved in
- the strategies you used and what was good or not so good about each
- how well your action plan worked, any changes that were made and why the changes were necessary
- your awareness of your own contributions as well as that of others – stating how well people worked together
- the rights, roles and responsibilities of all involved
- any problems encountered and how they were solved – who suggested the solutions to problems
- what you and others learned from the activity
- who benefited from the activity and how
- what was achieved overall

- suggestions for any improvements that could be made if a similar activity was to be repeated.

You need to show that you took an active part in and made a valuable contribution to the event.

Remember to read your work through thoroughly before you hand it in.

A final point

Now put the finishing touches to your report. Make an attractive front cover stating the following:

- the name of your school/centre
- the centre number
- your name
- your candidate number
- the course – GCSE Citizenship Studies
- the title of your report.

Add one final page at the back for acknowledgements (list the people who helped you) and a bibliography (list any books, magazines, leaflets, websites, etc. from which you obtained information).

11 Exam techniques

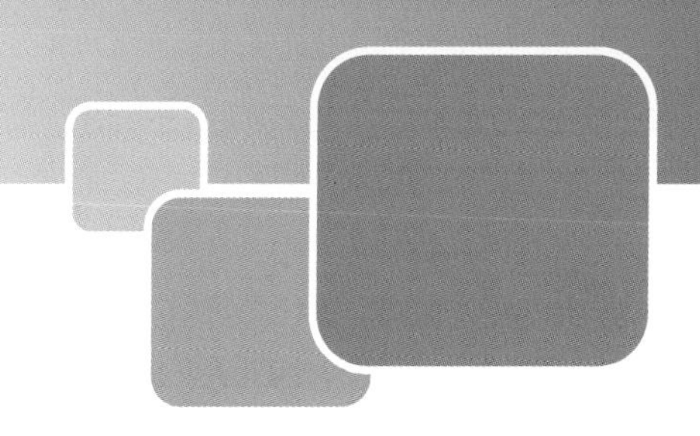

There is only one written paper for this course (there are no higher and foundation tiers) and it carries 60 per cent of the marks towards your exam grade.

There are no short cuts, only you can learn the work. Make yourself a revision plan. Set yourself targets and give yourself rewards when you achieve them. Everyone learns in a different way and by now you should know what suits you best.

The question paper

The question paper is divided into four sections: A, B, C and D. Each section is different in style, therefore different types of answers are required.

The exam paper will be in booklet form. You will be required to put your details on the front cover and answer the questions in the booklet. Read the instructions at the beginning of each section and follow them carefully. You will have one and a half hours (90 minutes) to complete the paper.

Section A

You must answer all the questions in this section. The questions are straightforward and need short factual answers. If you have been answering the questions at the end of each chapter, you should be familiar with this type of question (go back through these and test your knowledge). You should have no problem in answering any of the questions in this section.

The questions will cover all areas of the specification (syllabus).

Section B

In this section you must answer one compulsory source-based question divided into different parts. You must answer all parts of the question. The scenario may be taken from any area of the syllabus, and this will vary each year.

You will be given a short piece of text to read containing information about a situation. You will then be asked a question about the passage you have read, which will require you to make a judgement to show your understanding of the text – a type of comprehension question.

Another part of the question will ask you to use the information given and combine it with your own knowledge, for example on a community, a business or a world issue. You will be asked to write a response or determine what a possible outcome might be.

A further part of the question will require you to add your knowledge, form an opinion or describe who could influence the situation and how.

Section C

This section will contain one compulsory question divided into different parts. All parts of the question will relate to the citizenship activity you have taken part in for your coursework. You will be asked about your participation in the activity. You must answer all parts of the question.

This should be an easier section, as you should know more than anyone else about what you did.

Possible information you will be asked to provide includes:

- a good description or outline of your citizenship activity – include the aims or purpose of the activity
- an outline of how you planned the activity – think about any changes you made and your reasons for the changes and include these in the evaluation
- what your contribution was and your opinions on the activity
- how other people contributed to the activity and what their opinions were
- an assessment of how successful it was, who benefited from the activity, and who learned what
- how the activity could have been improved.

You could prepare answers to these questions as part of your revision, so that you are very familiar with them before the exam.

Note:
Read through your report on the activity as part of your exam revision.

Section D

In this section you will be asked to write an essay. You must choose one title from a choice of three.

All the essay titles will be from the themes that run throughout the course, that is:

- rights and responsibilities
- decision-making, power and authority
- participation in citizenship activities.

Guidance will be given about what you should include in your answer. These are not the only areas to cover but you should include all those mentioned and also apply your own knowledge to the subject.

Read all the essay titles and the suggested topics to include and make sure you understand what each one is asking. Now decide which one to tackle. Take a minute or two to think about your answer and what order you will put the topics in. Make a brief outline of the essay including what to put into each paragraph.

Now write the essay, remembering to justify any judgements you make. Present the facts and well-reasoned arguments, then state your opinion, which should be based on the knowledge you have displayed.

A final word

Plan your time wisely. Each section is worth the same number of marks so make sure you complete all parts of each section. When you have finished the paper, go back to the beginning and read each answer carefully, completing any parts that you have missed out. Check spelling and punctuation as a possible 6 marks for communication could be added to your total.

Whatever grade you achieve in Citizenship Studies, studying this course will have made you a more informed citizen. **Good luck!**

Glossary

Acid rain: Rain contaminated by chemicals from burning fuels

Advertising: Techniques used by to persuade consumers to buy goods

Agenda 21: Action plan for sustainable development agreed at Rio Summit (1992)

Aid programmes: Transfer of money, goods and expertise from one country to another

Authority: A form of power accepted as a legal right to rule

Budget: Economic statement about taxation and spending targets

Civil law: Relates to people's private rights, such as boundaries and marital breakdown

Commonwealth: Nations formerly known as the British Empire

Community: All the people who live or work in an area

Consumer: Person buying goods or services

Contract of employment: Written document containing terms conditions of employment

Crime: Any illegal or unlawful act against property or people

Criminal law: Relates to crimes against people or property

Culture: Shared language, behaviour, traditions and values of a society

Deforestation: Felling trees to make wood and paper products

Development gap: Divide between two-thirds of the world's population living in poverty and the other one-third living in plenty

Devolution: Transfer or delegation of power to regional level

Discrimination: Treating people less favourably than others because of their gender, ethnicity, religion or level of ability

Economy: How goods, services and finances are provided and managed

Ecosystem: Relationship between rocks, soils, vegetation, living organisms, water, atmosphere and climate

Equal opportunities: Fair treatment without discrimination

Ethnic identity: Particular culture of a group within society

European Convention on Human Rights (ECHR): Identifies citizens' human rights

European Union (EU): group of 15 states trading labour, goods and services in single market

Fairtrade: Trade organizations giving suppliers a reasonable price for their goods

Finance: Money raised for development through taxation or borrowing

Free trade: Use of low-priced raw materials and labour to create profit for multinational companies

Freedom of speech: The idea that people should be able to air their opinions without punishment

Global warming: Climate change caused by industrial gases which destroy the protective ozone layer and expose the Earth to increased heat

Government: Democratically elected members of parliament who set taxes to pay for public services and make laws for everyone to live by

Health and safety at work: Responsibilities of employers and employees to ensure safe working practices

Human rights: Include rights to liberty, justice, privacy, education and freedom

Industry: Businesses involving raw materials/natural resources, or manufactured products, or services

Law-making: Parliamentary process for designing new rules

Local government: System of councils responsible for looking after people, services and facilities in a county or urban area

Media: Newspapers, books and magazines, radio, television and video, advertising, cinema and the Internet

Multinational companies: Any free-trade business spread over several countries to keep costs low and profits high

North Atlantic Treaty Organization (NATO): Alliance of 13 countries committed to each others' defence

Political parties: People sharing the same views who try to win elections

Poverty: Insufficient food, clothing, housing, water and sanitation, and medical care

Power: The ability to influence or to rule

Pressure groups: People who join together to influence or change government policy

Racism: Treating people less favourably because they are from a different race

Religion: System of values and beliefs

Responsibilities: Duties towards oneself and others

Rights: Freedoms to which one is entitled

School community: A number of people working and learning together sharing the same values and rules

Sustainable development: Meeting the needs of the present without compromising the needs of the future

Taxation: Money taken from citizens by the government to finance public services

Third World: Countries with living standards, high birth and death rates, high infant mortality and low life expectancy

Trade: Any system for buying and selling goods and services

Trade unions: Collection of workers who join together to promote their common interests

United Nations (UN): Organization set up after World War II to promote international peace, security and co-operation

Voluntary organisations: Support groups who raise funds for and awareness of specific community issues or special groups

Voting: Citizens' opportunity to decide who should govern them

World Trade Organization (WTO): Free trade organization regulating import and export of goods between countries

Index